May 13 '80

"The detective quality of this strong memoir is both maddening and fascinating. The reader is made to feel what it's like to be denied answers in an essential search."

—AMY HEMPEL, *Sing to It*

"Atlantis Black was—is?—an extraordinary woman whose descent into madness will leave you spellbound and heartbroken. Betsy Bonner writes with the precision of a poet and the courage of a survivor. I could not put this book down."

—DOMENICA RUTA, *With or Without You*

"Scrappy and queer, charismatic and enigmatic, the young musician who reinvented herself as Atlantis Black left behind a haunting archive that complicates rather than resolves the narrative of her vibrant, troubled life. In this beautiful exploration of her sister's life and disappearance, Betsy Bonner has crafted a terse, urgent page-turner that is equally ode, elegy, and mystery."

—CHELSEY JOHNSON, *Stray City*

"Her manic, self-destructive sister wanted to be famous, but it took Betsy Bonner's literary gifts to make her a rock star on the page. In mournful, meticulous—and sometimes wryly funny—prose, *The Book of Atlantis Black* gives us an unforgettable portrait of an impossible yet compelling young woman taken down by her own demons, and fighting every step of the way."

—DAVID GATES, *A Hand Reached Down to Guide Me*

THE BOOK OF ATLANTIS BLACK

THE BOOK OF
ATLANTIS BLACK

THE SEARCH FOR A SISTER GONE MISSING

A MEMOIR BY

BETSY BONNER

 TIN HOUSE / Portland, Oregon

Published by Tin House, Portland, Oregon

Distributed by W. W. Norton & Company

Library of Congress Cataloging-in-Publication Data is available

First US Edition 2020
Printed in the USA
Interior design by Diane Chonette

www.tinhouse.com

for Queen Leah, dearest of cats (1999–2019)

and for David, with love and gratitude

Let *me* go, if you want me to let you in!

—EMILY BRONTË, *Wuthering Heights*

AUTHOR'S NOTE

The sections headed "San Diego, March 2008" were transcribed from a videotaped interview with my sister, Nancy, who had changed her name to Atlantis Black. This interview took place three months before she disappeared.

ONE

Can we turn the camera off? It's so cold.

1.

On June 25, 2008, a young woman with my sister's IDs was found dead on the floor of a hotel room in Tijuana. Her body had needle marks in the left arm, a wound on the right middle finger, and a bruised cranium. She wore blue jeans and a brown T-shirt that read GOOD KARMA. Two syringes were in the room: one on the nightstand, one in her purse. The police report said that the IDs— including an American passport and a California driver's license issued to "Eunice Atlantis Black"—did not appear to match the body, which was cremated without anyone's taking fingerprints or checking dental records. The autopsy report said the woman had green eyes and weighed less than one hundred pounds. It estimated her age to be twenty to twenty-five years old. The cause of death was a pancreatic hemorrhage.

My sister had hazel eyes, like my mother's. She was thirty-one and running from felony charges in a prescription drug case in the state of California when she disappeared.

By the time I heard the news, the only thing that might have shocked me would have been if my sister had found a way to live.

Just in case of some miraculous mistake, I called Atlantis's phone—
it seemed to be on—and left a voicemail message. Then I typed an
email: "Call me as soon as you can if you receive this. I love you." I
had no expectation of hearing back from her.

2.

In the summer of 2002, Atlantis took the stage, shook back the dark, straight hair that fell to her waist, and lifted the strap of an electric guitar over her shoulder. The instrument settled low on her hips. Strumming some quick minor chords, she tossed her head like a horse assailed by flies. Her silver-sequin tank top screamed Chinatown. A bony knee poked through her jeans as she leaned into the microphone and whispered, "Check." She made a hand motion as if to say: *Come here*. "Check," she said again, louder.

She said something inaudible to the pleasant-faced, leather-clad man climbing the stage, who nodded and took a seat behind the drum kit.

"Let's have a little more vocals," she said.

Bar chatter faded as Atlantis's husky voice filled the room. The cash register opened and shut.

"Check, check, check," she said. "That sounds great. Hey there, everyone! I'm Atlantis Black. Thank you all for coming out and braving the subways on such a swelteringly hot and humid New York City night. Thank you to the SideWalk Café for welcoming me into your extremely prestigious Antifolk Festival. Honest to God, if I didn't feel so fucking proud, I'd be a nervous wreck. Thank you to Regina Spektor for that ridiculously fabulous set, and to Lach for believing in me and inviting me here. So tonight I've got a few new goth surf rock tunes for you, some from my first album, *In My Bed*, and a couple of covers. This first one goes out to my little sister, Betsy, who's here tonight."

Most people assumed that I was the older sister, though I was two years younger. I was clearly the more serious and responsible one. I went to graduate school for poetry and had never been caught breaking the law; Atlantis used her mug shot from 1996 for an album cover. (She'd taken hallucinogens with a friend in the Mojave Desert. I don't know what they did to get busted for "public intoxication.")

The drummer tapped off sticks, and Atlantis built a tower of minor chords. When it threatened to topple into noise, he knocked it down, and Atlantis picked up the shards. Her voice echoed as if from the innermost whorl of a shell:

pour the hot wax on my skin
you always were my sweetest sin

In the middle of a riff, the tank top strap slipped from Atlantis's shoulder, and her right breast popped out of her shirt like a pale, trembling Chihuahua. Some girls in crew cuts cheered. The Chihuahua twitched its dark nose. I sucked down the rest of my Maker's and ginger.

"You're awesome!" yelled a kid with orange hair, raising his thin, muscular arms.

She finished the song, then pulled up her tank top strap as if it were no big deal.

"Wow," she said. "That was quite . . . cathartic. This next one's called: 'Another Fucked-Up Beauty Queen.'"

It was impossible for me to judge Atlantis's music critically. Her riot grrrl songs were inspired by punk and goth bands that we both liked; she was allergic to pretty radio voices. Her themes were sex, drugs, and a love of pain, death, and transformation. She often sang from the perspective of a spurned lover, with lyrics addressed to an unattainable "you," and ending on a tragic note. Her songs were easier to listen to when they were more playful and ironic, like "I Can't Kill Myself Today." A tribute to her vibrator, "My Machine," had gotten a mention in *Time Out New York*.

Before Atlantis performed a song, she practiced it for months. If she played a wrong note, she went back to the place where it still sounded good and tried again. She was the most obsessive artist I've ever known.

Atlantis used to say that classical piano relaxed her more than any other music. She didn't like violins (too screechy), symphonies (too boring and too much), or electronic music (no soul). Yet she never tried to pick up piano herself.

Our mother was a skilled pianist and as a teenager had performed weekly in church. Growing up, I asked Mom to teach me piano on the spinet her mother had taught her on, and I practiced a lot. Sometimes when I got a little loud, or maybe when she grew tired of hearing me, Mom would say, "Light touch." I thought she laughed to herself after saying it; it was probably something she'd been told when she was learning. Atlantis would never have tolerated musical criticism from Mom.

In my sophomore year of college, I studied piano with Edmund Niemann, who played with Steve Reich's ensemble and wrote music for Meredith Monk. He taught me to play some classical pieces that became Atlantis's favorites. Whenever we were both at home, she'd beg me to play Chopin, Brahms, and Beethoven, which she said had goth riffs.

After college, when I lived with Atlantis in New York, I bought a keyboard with headphones and recorded songs I made up late at night. I could play only when I was certain that no one but God himself was listening—not the neighbors, not Atlantis.

The first time I saw Atlantis onstage—she was still called Nancy then—she was a high school freshman playing Shakespeare's Juliet. In the dark auditorium, I watched her die. She was a great actress, especially convincing when it came to representing pain. After that, I became an actress, too, a Miranda marveling at a "brave new world, / That has such people in't."

I believed that the demons possessing Atlantis would kill her if she didn't perform. But I worried that she might actually become famous. I worried for both of us.

3.

Nancy and I grew up in Wyeth country: Chadds Ford, Pennsylvania. The painter Andrew Wyeth's family lived three miles east across the highway, in the historic district. Where we lived, on Hillendale Road, there were beautiful woods and sweet old stone farmhouses, side by side with kitschy 1950s ranches and 1960s housing developments. Working-class country folks lived next door to wealthy horse people and nouveau riche commuters to Philadelphia; almost everyone was white. Our house was a split-level, painted and maintained by my father. The closest businesses were a mile and a half away: a gas station, a diner called Hank's Place, and the Wawa food market, where my father took us every Sunday after Mass and permitted Nancy and me one candy bar each. In the summer, before I learned to drive, I walked in the woods, read books, watched TV, and hung out with Nancy and a few friends who lived nearby. Sometimes we went swimming or tubing where the Brandywine River narrowed to a creek. There was a scary rope swing over the black rocks and waterfalls that we loved.

Chadds Ford was named for a businessman, John Chads—the town fathers didn't pay much attention to spelling—who opened a ferry service across the Brandywine River in the late 1730s. The Leni Lenape had presumably forded that river for thousands of years before he arrived. When I was growing up, a few Native Americans still lived in the area, some of whom sat for Andrew Wyeth, the only artist I was aware of; my parents displayed framed prints of his drawings and paintings around our house. On my way up the stairs to their room—where I sometimes found my mother during the day—I was both mesmerized and spooked by the figure in *The Berry Picker*: with two brimming baskets and boyish, short hair that frames a face turned away from the viewer, the berry picker appears to be napping in the afternoon. For a long time I thought the figure was a young man until I noticed the small breasts under the loose white shirt.

In October 1945, Wyeth's father, Newell Convers Wyeth, known for his illustrations of *Robinson Crusoe* and *Treasure Island*, died on the railroad tracks where the Octoraro line crossed Ring Road, a few miles from where our house would be built. When I was growing up, the story I heard was that his car stalled on the tracks and was hit by a train. In the 1940s, some trains still carried passengers on the line, but it was most likely a freight that killed N. C. and his four-year-old grandson. A Wilmington, Delaware, newspaper dated October 19, 1945, read: "Troopers Believe Famous Painter Was Blinded by Sun as He Drove Up Incline toward Tracks." David Michaelis's biography of N. C. Wyeth suggests that the accident might have been a suicide.

Less than a year after what the newspapers called a "double tragedy," Andrew Wyeth painted *Winter 1946*, a figure that he described as "almost tumbling down a hill across a strong winter light, with his hand flung wide and a black shadow racing behind him, and bits of snow, and my feeling of being disconnected from everything. It was me, at a loss—that hand drifting in the air was my free soul, groping. Over on the other side of that hill was where my father was killed, and I was sick I'd never painted him." But would he have been any less grief-stricken if he had?

I wonder the same thing about writing this book.

When I first heard PJ Harvey's album Rid of Me, *I heard what I had never heard in my life. It was a woman screaming, but not in like an L7 way. It was real. And it was produced very finely—I heard a woman rasping. Almost like gasping for air.*

The next day I got out and bought every album that was available. I liked the whispering, the groaning, the lo-fi-ness. I was like, You know what, I can do that.

4.

Nancy was my canary, ahead of me in the dark.

Our mother was manic-depressive and suicidal, so Nancy and I were raised mostly by our father. He was a conservative Catholic, and he had rules for us. No frivolous adornments. No best-friend necklaces, because to accept one might hurt another little girl's feelings. I had to give back at least two broken hearts to confused friends. No ear piercings until the magic age—thirteen. After confirmation, we would be free to wear what we wanted. But if we chose whorish things, God couldn't save us from falling into hell.

At church and at Catholic school, I loved to think of Jesus in the stations of the cross—how he climbed the hill and fell under his burden; climbed some more and fell again; climbed and fell a third time, turning the other cheek to his torturers. I saw how his performance of suffering, humiliation, and death led him to rise in ecstasy. God's love meant being above it all. To endure pain would earn me transformation too: in others' eyes, and in the life to come.

·

When the devil—often in the form of Nancy—tempted me to do something bad and fun, I usually managed to get away with it. In confession, I learned how to lie in an honest voice. Like most Catholic children, if I couldn't think of anything to tell, I invented wrongdoings that would elicit the penance of a few Hail Marys.

Nancy seldom did what she was told; nor did she attempt to hide her disobedience. Our father tried to beat her into submission with brutal spankings on her bare skin, and threatened her with his belt, though I don't remember seeing him hit her with it. He wasn't drunk; he just flew into rages, especially over his firstborn, little Nancy, who looked a bit like his sister—she'd died of breast cancer when we were children—and who definitely looked like our mother. For years, I believed that such abuse was normal—and it was, in the families I knew, most of whom went to the same church we did.

·

Nancy was an ingenious mimic. One evening, when we were both less than ten years old, she wrapped herself in our father's gray cotton bathrobe and pretended to be Father Walker, our parish priest. She went to the kitchen and opened a bag of Wonder Bread; with her fists, she flattened slices on the counter, unscrewed a two-liter bottle of Coke, and used the cap to make circular impressions in the bread. I helped her pile up the wafers. She snatched a glass and a bottle of grape juice and led me to her bedroom, where she draped a sheet over her desk, told me to kneel on the floor next to it, and, with nail-bitten fingers, fed me the body of Christ. Then our father came in and pushed me out of the room. I heard horrible thudding sounds. Later, Nancy told me that he had her by the hair, and those sounds I heard were of him slamming her head into the wall between our rooms. It wouldn't shock me if he had damaged my sister's brain, long before any drugs she was prescribed or used for comfort.

When he went onto the back porch to smoke a cigarette, Nancy crawled out of her room, went to the kitchen phone, and called the police to report child abuse. Mom got up off the couch—she'd been watching TV—and took the phone out of her hand. "Don't come here," she said to the person on the other end. "My girls were just playing." She put the phone in its cradle and told Nancy, "You have to stop setting off your father."

A police officer came anyway. Officer Peach talked to each of my family members individually and told Nancy and me that we should call again if anything happened.

.

Every autumn, our school closed for the first day of hunting season. From deep in the game preserve across the road, the sound of gun- shots echoed off the beautifully maintained colonial farmhouses, and off our 1950s-style ranch. Though our father warned us not to venture too far into the woods alone and without wearing bright colors, I was drawn by the sun-bleached bones—deer, rabbits, and squirrels—that I found there. I considered myself an amateur natu- ralist. Sometimes I followed Nancy along the ATV trails to a birch- branch fort that other children had built. As we moved through the forest, we pretended we were outlaws, pantomiming a shoot-out. Sometimes I was a doe, and she nailed me.

•

There were signs that Nancy was different from the other children I knew. She ate sparingly, and whenever I drank milk, she insisted that the bluish traces at the bottom of the glass were "cow veins." I told myself she was crazy, but I also thought she might have psychic powers.

•

I was six and Nancy was eight when I first heard that she had been molested. It was one of the few times she knocked on my bedroom door without opening it. I remember her freckled face covered with tears. She said that our next-door neighbor, a teenage boy, made her give him blow jobs, and put his fingers inside her. I didn't understand what she was talking about. She wanted him to stop, but was afraid he'd get mad and that no one would believe her anyway, since his dad was buddies with the sheriff. I advised her to tell our babysitter. When she finally did, our babysitter—who went to high school with him—said: "He dates *senior* girls."

But Nancy's claim was plausible. Since our next-door neighbor boy helped our family take care of the yard, he had easy access to our house, garage, and toolshed. One friend and neighbor, Tara, remembers him and Nancy "hugging" in the backyard while we were all playing hide-and-seek. Tara was a year younger than me and looked up to my sister at least as much as I did. At the time, she told me years later, a romance with an older boy seemed cool, and to see him holding Nancy in secret only made her worship Nancy more. Of course, what Tara saw suggests that they might have had a relationship even more disturbing than a single predatory attack.

.

Once, when Nancy was thirteen, she climbed out of her window in the middle of the night and walked the nine miles to our school, through woods and fields and across Highway 1. My parents assumed that she had spent the night at a girlfriend's and didn't seem worried about her absence. The next day, she showed up on time for her environmental science class and took her seat near where a buck's head poked out of the wall. She told me she couldn't sleep anyway, and that night-walking was a beautiful and tranquilizing experience that I should try sometime.

Not long afterward, though, Nancy cut her wrists and lay down in her waterbed. I'm not sure who found her bleeding, maybe our father. We went together as a family to see a psychiatrist. Nancy said that nightmares—in which she felt as if she were being choked to death—made it impossible for her to sleep. The psychiatrist prescribed the antidepressant Paxil. After that, when Nancy said she felt sick, she refused to take the school bus in the morning and our parents let her stay home.

.

Nancy liked to taunt Mr. Heller, a history teacher who worked in the attendance office. She was convinced that he was a sexual predator, though she never said how she knew—she just did. She gave him excuse notes that she'd obviously written herself with our mother's forged signature; she knew that Mom didn't want to be bothered and would confirm that her daughter was sick. After Nancy racked up more than the twenty absences permitted without a doctor's note, our father was required to appear in court. Years later, she mailed me a newspaper clipping about the history teacher. She'd drawn devil horns on the head of Roger Heller, who had pleaded guilty to sexually abusing the teenage female manager of the basketball team. He would spend six months behind bars. Above the head she'd written "Oi towld yew!" in the phonetic spelling we used to indicate the speech of our low-life neighbors.

.

When we were teenagers—and later, in our twenties, when we shared apartments in New York City—my sister would come into my bedroom, lie down on the floor, and start talking. She told me she believed in reincarnation, and that she felt attracted to the desert because her spirit animal was a coyote. She asked if I had experienced astral projection, and when I said I hadn't she told me I'd have to be lying down and hovering at the edge of a dream. I didn't envy Nancy's out-of-body experiences—she'd earned them, I thought, by her suffering; and most of the time I liked being in my own skin.

.

Sometimes Nancy would chase me with a kitchen knife until I fled to my bedroom, and would drag the knife down my door in long strokes, ruining the paint. The barrier between us felt thin as cardboard. "Pig," she would whisper, as if in a trance. "Gonna slit you open, slit you open. Right through your little pink stomach." It might have been funny, but it wasn't—not with my little pink stomach. Fleet, nimble Nancy tackled me easily when she actually wanted to hurt me. In the piggy-knife game, she didn't want to catch me.

．

If you could add up the hours, we must have spent weeks studying our own images in the mirror between our twin sinks. Sometimes, when she caught me copying her while she was curling her hair, or applying heavy eyeliner, she'd say: "Don't look." If I kept looking, she commanded my reflection: "I said don't *look* at me." When I still looked, she raised the curling iron, singed her hair-sprayed bangs, and made a terrible burning smell.

．

Nancy got her first period only shortly before I got mine, hers at age fourteen and a half, mine at thirteen. I saw that she bound her pads tightly in toilet paper, like the feet of royal Chinese ladies, before putting them back in their plastic sleeves and disposing of them. I followed suit, out of shame over the blood and the odor.

One winter afternoon, Nancy and I had both taken Advil and were sharing her heated double waterbed. She was listening to Sheryl Crow on headphones; I was reading *Jane Eyre*. Mom knocked loudly on Nancy's bedroom door and asked us to come into the living room.

I was surprised to see the bathroom wastebasket sitting on top of the coal-burning stove. When we walked in, she overturned it, and down rained a dozen or so sanitary napkins that Nancy and I had thrown away. Mom's hands trembled, and I thought she was having a manic episode.

"So girls: you don't need to wrap up your—uh—*things* in toilet paper. Just use the plastic they come in."

"Oh my God," Nancy said.

"I had to use a rag, you know, and wash it out every night. Also, you're changing them too frequently. See—"

She picked up one of our "things," took it out of the plastic, unwrapped it like a mummy, and displayed it. "Someone barely used this."

"Ew! You're nasty," Nancy said. "Come on, Betsy."

"You girls are wastrels," Mom called after us.

.

In middle school, Nancy and I bought paperbacks at Pathmark, the nearest grocery store—a twenty-minute drive—and got every book by V. C. Andrews. In those books, intercourse meant incest and female sacrifice. Mom called them "trash." The Heaven Leigh Casteel series, where poor Heaven lives in a hillbilly town with some nasty folks, was my favorite; I blushed at the word *languorous*. Nancy preferred *My Sweet Audrina*, which features an abused girl, in a rocking chair, with a Swiss cheese memory.

.

In high school, Nancy started having sex with Dave, who was a couple of years older and went to the poorer school nearby in Kennett Square. He also had a girlfriend, Crystal, who used more hair product than the girls at Unionville-Chadds Ford. When Crystal found out what Nancy was up to, she phoned our house with death threats.

"Don't pick up," Nancy said, as the phone rang and rang.

"What's sex like?" I asked.

"It kills," Nancy said.

"So why do you do it?"

"Dave wanted to," she said.

"Heather *likes* boffing. She says it feels good."

Heather, my best friend, went to an all-girls Catholic school and was the only kid I knew who knew as much about sex as Nancy.

"Don't use that dumb word. God, you sound so stupid. It's like being ripped in half, okay? You can't even begin to imagine the pain."

I thought she was basking in her secret knowledge.

"Isn't that just the first time?" I said.

"No. *Every single time.* Dave says I'm small, though. You might be okay."

At thirteen, I longed to get as close to sex as I could without actually losing my virginity. When Nancy mentioned that a new boyfriend (after Dave) had a younger brother, we went swimming at their house every day. I spent the summer after eighth grade making out with that boy in his finished basement, while Nancy had sex upstairs.

·

When Nancy turned sixteen, our father offered to buy her a car, and she chose a used white Alfa Romeo convertible. She asked me to photograph her in it. She wore lipstick, a violet T-shirt, white jean shorts with a metal belt, and flip-flops. She had a little brush in her pocket and fixed her hair between shots. When she got out of the car, I thought we were done, but she told me to wait. Right there in the driveway, she stripped to her underwear and put on a tighter shirt, long jeans, and black boots she'd stashed under the seat. She climbed up on the hood and stood with her hands on her hips. Then she lay down on the hood, propped herself up on her elbows, and gazed into the distance. Once she started to laugh and said, "Hold on." It was hard for her to stop smiling in pictures.

.

Nancy never seemed interested in eventually having a husband, children, a house—the things most girls in our town considered essential. Instead she wanted fame, and she got it: in a limited, local way. By the time she was a teenager, she began to acquire a pack of friends, many of them boys with long hair who went to Kennett. Popular kids—jocks and snobs—called her and her friends "heathens." Nancy became the girl who could drink boys under the table at parties and still stay skinny enough to walk out of a department store in two pairs of jeans.

Somewhere there's a photograph of the mountain of stolen gifts she piled in her room before surprising our family one Christmas; she gave me a pair of Anne Klein sunglasses with tiny golden lion heads on the stems. One summer when she wanted an electric fan, she simply picked up a floor model at Kmart and walked out with it. Her rules about stealing were clear in her mind. It was not cool to take from an individual person, like the Indian woman who sold jewelry from a cart in the mall. On the other hand, it was highly ethical to steal from big businesses and corporations.

Just once, when she was sixteen, Nancy got caught, by a security manager at Strawbridge's. She flirted with him in his office; he decided not to call the police, and let her go.

SAN DIEGO, MARCH 2008

I wrote eighty-some songs in an apartment in LA circa 1995. I loved the weather, but I hated LA — it was not conducive to my being a performer. So I moved to New York and lived there for about six years. I love New York, and that's where I really got the band together. It started out as myself with an acoustic guitar. But then it started metamorphosing into this giant carnival thing. I recorded my first EP, self-produced, in 2002. It was entirely analog. I prefer analog to Garage Band. Digital—you can get it on any Mac. My first album sounds real gritty, but I like the grit. I like the grit a lot.

5.

In 360 BCE, when Plato invented the lost island of Atlantis in his dialogues *Timaeus* and *Critias*, most readers understood that it was not a real place. But in 1882, Ignatius Donnelly, a politician from Philadelphia, published *Atlantis: The Antediluvian World*, a pseudoscientific account of Atlantis's flora, fauna, and history. The theosophists Madame Blavatsky and Rudolf Steiner expanded the mythology and wrote about Atlanteans as a "root race" that actually existed ten thousand years ago. Blavatsky's *The Secret Doctrine* (1888) described Atlanteans as godlike beings who had become human and thereby destroyed themselves. They had psychic powers (telepathy, astral projection) and advanced technology but suffered from hubris, practiced "black magic," and drowned in a catastrophic flood. Steiner's *Atlantis and Lemuria* (1904) claimed that Atlanteans existed in a kind of "dream consciousness" and valued personal experience over traditional learning: an Atlantean "did not think, he remembered." Despite the use of "he," Steiner conceived of Atlanteans as genderless: "It had become possible for their souls to fertilize themselves with mind, without waiting for the development of the inner organs of the human physical body."

In 1994, my seventeen-year-old sister, with the artistry and self-generation of a true Atlantean, gave birth to a new self; for Atlantis Black to exist, she had to get rid of Eunice Anne Bonner. She never went back to high school. She got her GED and was accepted to Loyola University in New Orleans—she'd set her heart on that city for its musical soul—and said that no one with such a boring name as Bonner would ever make it there. Our father thought this was a slight against our Irish ancestors and initially refused to sign the necessary papers. But my sister was his first child, the one he preferred both to please and to harm, and she was persistent. Two local newspapers printed the legal notice, and the people of Chadds Ford had a month to make known any objections. There were none. Eunice Anne Bonner drove herself to the hearing and emerged Eunice Anne Black. It cost more money to change both names, she said, and getting rid of Bonner took precedence. ("The Boner girls," boys called us.) Later on, she forged the original document to make Atlantis (not Anne) her middle name. I never knew how she came to choose the name, but it seems perfect: the Atlantis of legend is mystical, self-destroying, and forever lost.

I learned this thing with my voice that I didn't do in my early music. Instead of just being all wispy, I started to do more inflections. I just made sure it was in tune. I got that from Tori Amos. She—Tori—and I grew up in a similar way. I grew up with that fucking Irish Catholic guilt. I had to go to Catholic school. Actually, I probably have a lot more in common with Madonna. She influenced me incredibly.

People accused me of fucking my guitar. I say, well, if you're over the top, then you've therefore created a new apex for being the top. I get a lot of heat from one particular song called "I'll Take What I Can Get." It begins:

danger's such a beautiful thing
you look so pretty when you come
all over me
all over me

There are always people in the audience who chuckle or shut up or both.
Another one, "Parking Lot Queen," goes:

hand job queen
my sweetest dream
bring it over for the team
yeah, yeah
for the team

I write about reality. That's what it's like for a sixteen-year-old girl who
wants to escape the misogyny of her small town. It makes me a little
nervous, though, whenever I play at a new venue that I've never played
at. I get nervous and—

6.

The year Atlantis left home, my high school science teacher took our class into the woods to identify birds. European starlings, he told us, usurp the nests of scarcer native birds, like chickadees. Best to kill them on the spot. He scooped up an imaginary bird and twisted its neck.

I had become an outspoken student with a passion for animal rights, and a touch of snobbishness. Back in the classroom, I told my teacher that his attitude about starlings was "speciesist"—a term I'd learned by reading Peter Singer's *Animal Liberation*—and cruel. If I wanted to talk about cruelty, he said, what about the starlings? They didn't just steal nests but pecked out the baby birds' eyes.

.

One night at dinner, I announced that I'd chosen to write a thirty-page paper rather than dissect a cat; a friend and I were the only students in our class to demand an alternative. My father laughed and called me an asshole. I said that it took a "real fat asshole" of a human being not to think about the damage he caused to the planet just to satisfy his enormous gut. He called me "rotten," and I said what was "rotten" was the animal carcass on the dinner table— and flung a forkful of spaghetti at him. He jumped out of his chair, pinned me to the kitchen floor, gripped my hair, and slammed my head against the linoleum. Mom told him to stop but didn't dare to intervene physically. I horse-kicked him in the stomach, and he let go of my hair. Both of us were astonished.

I didn't bother to call Officer Peach, who'd showed my sister and me long before how useless the police were. I stayed with a friend's family for most of the following summer, and talked on the phone with Atlantis, who was loving life in New Orleans. I told her what had happened, that I was too old for this and didn't think I could forgive Dad. She said I didn't have to. My liberation, she promised, would come in the form of a driver's license.

·

During Atlantis's first semester at Loyola, she'd found work as a waitress at a strip club. In her second semester, she dropped out and moved to Los Angeles. College wasn't very interesting, she said, and she wanted to focus on making music. I was worried when she told me that she'd taken yet another name—Roxanne—for a phone sex job, but she said it was the easiest money she'd ever made in her life, and that none of the girls took it seriously.

·

Chris was twenty-one, gorgeous, fresh out of Swarthmore College, and the youngest teacher our school had ever hired. He was the first teacher who lent me books from his private collection: Sylvia Plath, James Baldwin, and Anne Sexton. I told my friend Tara that I was in love.

"Oh, Betsy, no!" she said. "He's so gay!"

"He mentioned a girlfriend in Wilmington," I said.

"That's just so the jocks won't kill him."

All year, I tried to entice Chris with my purple prose, wishing he would deflower me—a word and concept I'd gotten from V. C. Andrews. He left Unionville after a year and went on to have a successful writing career; but he stayed in touch and recommended me to my first-choice colleges.

·

In trigonometry class I noticed a boy named Greg, who had silky blond hair and a Pearl Jam T-shirt. After five months of making out, I told him I wanted my first time to be with him, in my childhood bed, with no condom. After my deflowering we'd be more prudent. Greg said that sounded great.

When we'd been having sex for a few months, Greg's mother called and invited my mother to lunch and told her she'd found a condom wrapper on her son's floor.

"Well," Mom said, "at least they're using protection."

I'd wanted Greg and me to apply to the same colleges, but I discovered that he hadn't applied to any of my top choices, as he'd said he had. I learned that he was cheating on me with a girl who went to private school.

I called Atlantis in Los Angeles and told her about my broken heart. There was something wrong with most men, she said, and this proved it. She didn't want to tell me sooner because she knew I'd been in love; and she was only now figuring things out herself. She confided in me that Dana, one of her female neighbors, was teaching her how to have sex with women. Photocopies of work by Andrea Dworkin and Catharine MacKinnon showed up in the mailbox, addressed to me in Atlantis's serial-killer handwriting.

·

In my last month of senior year, Atlantis called from a pay phone in Albuquerque and said she was on her way home. She'd had it with Los Angeles. She'd yelled at a guy who was getting disgusting on the phone, and told him she was a three-hundred-pound lesbian, and that he must have a tiny dick. She'd pawned everything she could and would be home in three days. She needed a free place to live and hoped to earn some quick cash in Chadds Ford before moving to New York.

Three days later, I came home from school, saw the Alfa in the driveway, and found Atlantis sacked out in the living room, with a Cybill Shepherd movie on the TV.

In the year and a half since we'd seen each other, she'd grown her hair to her waist. She wore the same heavy eyeliner and mascara whose application she'd perfected in high school, but no foundation, blush, or lipstick—just a thin dusting of powder. She was still enviably thin.

"You look good," I said.

"It's the desert," she said. "You have to go there. The dry heat is amazing—actually clears up your skin. There's no humidity. And everyone is happy and nice to other people. It's nothing like Chadds Ford."

"What do people *do* in the desert?"

"Whatever they want. It's like a lot of small communities, Native Americans and cool people who don't like mainstream society. Actually, though, of all the places I've been, you'd love Northern California. You applied to Stanford, right?"

"I'm going to Sarah Lawrence," I said. "They offered me a small scholarship."

"What, are *you* a dyke now?" she said. "What's it cost after the scholarship?"

"Expensive," I said.

"Is Dad paying for it?"

"He said he would. I'm taking out loans. You know," I said, "you might want to consider a liberal arts college. Dad would pay for you again, and you could study music or something you're actually interested in."

"I'm not going back," she said. "Oh, I have something for you."

The laminated card she put in my hand said Atlantis Black was born in 1974—two years before her actual birth—and had black hair and brown eyes. The photograph showed her tilting her head down to hide the Irish double chin she'd inherited from our father. She no longer needed that particular ID, she said, and I could use it if I ever wanted to go out in Philadelphia or New York. I shouldn't worry about the eye color—which was a mistake anyway—because no one ever checked in the dark. We still looked alike, mostly because of our long, dark hair, which we wore loose down our backs.

I told her I didn't care about bars, and certainly didn't want to get caught sneaking into one.

"It must be nice to be so straight," she said. "You better keep it just in case."

·

She talked her way into a telemarketing job, which earned her more money than most nineteen-year-olds made in our town. I had no idea how she spent her time when she wasn't at work until I came home one afternoon from rehearsing *The Diary of Anne Frank*, a school production in which the English teacher had created a position for me—assistant director!—and caught her at the living room window, peering through binoculars at one of our new neighbors, a fourteen-year-old girl, next door.

The Girl Next Door was in her yard by the wading pool, playing with her kid sister. Like a little mother, she lifted her sister up and out of the water, and then dunked her back in. We lived close enough to hear their screen door open and close, and when their mom came out in chino shorts carrying a tray of snacks and lemonade, I saw Atlantis's body tense. I watched her watching their mom set the tray by the pool's edge and open her arms to the child in the water. The Girl Next Door threw a towel in their direction and curled into a sagging lawn chair with a dELiA*s catalog.

"Do you think she's straight?" my sister said.

"They are all straight," I said.

"She has wicked thighs," she said.

"She's in eighth grade," I said.

"On the cusp of teenage dreams. Doesn't their mom look exactly like Lana Turner in *The Postman Always Rings Twice?*" In an attempt to distract ourselves from the humidity, we'd been staying up late watching the Bravo network.

I sneaked a peek at their mom's long, tanned legs myself. "You didn't even know who Lana Turner *was* until I told you."

"What color do you think her eyes are?" my sister said.

"Dunno. Brown hair, brown eyes, I guess."

"Wrong! She has black eyes."

"There's no such thing," I said.

"At her age, I was getting drunk and having sex with those assholes in the Burger King parking lot," Atlantis said. "I can't believe her mom lets her wear hot pants to school."

I tossed my *Sassy* magazine on the coffee table.

"I'm going to write her a letter," she said. "Something from the Wolf, to make her wet." Lately, she had become fixated on some entity that possessed her, which she called the Beast or the Wolf.

"She'll think it's from a guy," I said.

"Duh." She picked up her guitar. "I'll address it to her soul."

.

Every day for the next week, Atlantis waited for nightfall, then put on a bandit mask from Woolworth's and left love letters for the Girl Next Door in her family's mailbox. She typed them on our Brother word processor; she never let me read them in their entirety, but I often saw the word *princess*. Sometimes there was a rose pressed inside. It was bizarre, but I kept her secret. There didn't seem to be much else for me to do.

"But why her?" I asked her. To me, the Girl Next Door looked like a normal, shy, awkward young teenager.

"She's *astoundingly* beautiful. Are you blind?" When she was her age, Atlantis said, she would have loved to have gotten anonymous letters. They were perfectly harmless, they would make the Girl feel awesomely powerful, and they would raise her standards. Without someone or something to wake the Girl up, she'd probably get stuck with one of the dumb locals for a husband. She was too gorgeous to spend her life in Chadds Ford.

·

One day the Girl Next Door sat behind me on the school bus. I pretended to search for something in my bag, then turned and asked her if she had a pen. She looked up from her homework. Black eyes.

·

The point of the letters, Atlantis claimed, was to lift the Girl above the boring life that seemed destined for her. But of course she grew bored with her stalker game. She wanted to know what the Girl thought about the letters. Did they make her feel special? Did she have any suspects?

So she decided to confess. She wanted to do it in person and asked me to back her up. I was scared to go along—I didn't know if the father had a gun, as many of our neighbors did—but I didn't want her to do it alone.

When the mom came to the door, Atlantis asked to see the Girl.

"She's doing homework."

"Actually, we're wondering if we can borrow her yearbook," Atlantis said.

The mom closed the screen door and disappeared inside. After a couple of minutes, she came back. "She says she didn't get one this year."

"Well, what about a bike pump?" Atlantis said.

The mom folded her arms across her chest.

"Look," Atlantis said. "I'm the one writing letters to your daughter."

"Why are you telling me?" the mom said.

"She has to know," Atlantis said. "I thought she'd be flattered. Would you please just tell her that I didn't mean to scare her? And we can talk if she wants?"

"I think you two better get out of here," the mom said, and shut the door in our faces.

.

A few weeks before graduation, in the photography class darkroom, I met James, a new kid wearing a Marilyn Manson T-shirt. His family had moved to town from California. We started talking after school in the parking lot. I mentioned that my sister had just moved back from Los Angeles, and I asked him what California was like; the farthest west I'd ever been was Altoona, Pennsylvania. He asked if he could take pictures of me, and soon I had an arty, androgynous boyfriend.

.

That summer, Atlantis found a group of friends at Sisters, a lesbian bar in Philadelphia. She spent weekends away and came
home on Sunday afternoons tipsy and reeking of cigarette smoke.
Our father tried to rein us both in. He made rules for how late
Atlantis could stay out (which she ignored) and said that James
and I were no longer permitted to watch movies in my bedroom
with the door closed. I asked if Atlantis was still allowed to have
girls in her bedroom, or if this was just a ban on heterosexuality.
My father didn't understand what I meant, but my sister was furious. "I cannot believe you just did that to me, Betsy," she said, and
drove off in the Alfa.

She didn't speak to me for a couple of days—the longest fight
we had ever had—and when she finally broke her silence, I apologized for outing her to our father. I had meant to mock his bigotry
and I had assumed that everybody already knew about her sexual
preference. She told me it was the dumbest thing I'd ever done; our
father, along with most of our family, still believed that our cousin
Kathy's longtime partner was her roommate.

"Oh well," I said. "Soon enough, we'll both be living in New
York."

I had three close calls with three separate producers. This is what made me have a meltdown circa 2004–5. I was in touch with Mark Wallis, who produced U2 and Talking Heads. And then Ian Grimble, who produced Siouxsie and the Banshees and Travis. And then Steve Lyon, who produced Depeche Mode and the Cure. I settled on Steve Lyon because his repertoire was more similar to my style of music. I flew him out—he offered to record my songs for free. We blocked off four days to record my second album. The album—the album's title was gonna be More than Opium. *We recorded two songs. Then we got pummeled by a snowstorm in Pennsylvania to the point that the power went out. For four days. And then he had to fly to Portugal and Germany to record more famous people. And I was like,* Oh my God, my life is over. *I was having a personal issue at the time. It was very, very hard on me because I thought I had reached that pinnacle of where I wanted to be, and I thought I'd never be there again.*

7.

My mother, Marybeth Heffner, was salutatorian of her high school class and got a full scholarship to Dickinson College. She went on to get a master's in mathematics, then a PhD in communications from the University of Washington. My father, James Bonner, went from the army into business management, and to night school at Drexel University for his MBA. By the summer of 1975, they'd both ended up working at DuPont in Wilmington, Delaware; they got married the following January, and Nancy was born nine months later. My mother wanted children and didn't think she had much time left: she was thirty-four, and my father was forty, when they had Nancy.

.

Mom often napped in the afternoons, and sometimes, when her depression was bad, she would lie down in the pools of sunlight on the living room floor, moving her body a few inches an hour.

She looked like Wyeth's berry picker. But she seldom seemed to be asleep; rather, she was in the unrest of anxiety. She wore the same bathrobe, or the same faded cotton jumpsuit, for days on end.

Things were the opposite when she was manic: brassy colors in outlandish patterns swirled and clashed on her thin frame. She began reading, writing, gardening, and sewing projects—many of which she actually finished—and buzzed around the house like a motorboat without a pilot. Sometimes she shouted: "I hate kids!" and laughed her head off. Nancy, as she did with so many things, made it into a game. She taught me to shout back, in unison with her: "Then why did you have us?"

"I wanted to see what you'd look like," Mom said.

•

Mom read tarot cards on the sofa, and I noticed that she always put down the same card first: a woman who looked a bit like her, sitting on a throne with lions carved in the sides. She held a sunflower in one hand, a wand in the other, and had a black cat at her feet. Whenever she finished her reading, she offered to give me one. "Yes, please," I'd say, and inch closer to this woman I barely knew, but who fascinated me. She showed me the Queen of Cups, a good signifier for me, she said, since I was a water sign and a romantic. She told me to think of a question and then cut the cards. I had no idea what I wanted to know. Who would I marry? Where would I live? What would my daughters look and be like?

•

When I was five and Nancy was seven, Mom stopped sleeping with my father in the master bedroom and moved into Nancy's room, at the opposite end of the house and down a flight of stairs. At that time, Nancy's room had two twin beds, mine just one. It was a little strange that Mom didn't send me to Nancy's room and take over mine. Perhaps she and Nancy protected each other from my father's outbursts. It seemed like they were having a slumber party, but I didn't mind not being invited: Nancy and Mom both liked to stay up late talking, while I had my sleep and my privacy.

.

By 1984, Mom had asked my father for a divorce, which he refused her. He wrote her a letter saying that life without God was spiritual suicide and sent letters to her psychiatrist citing her failures as a wife, mother, and housekeeper. Nancy found carbon copies of those letters in his dresser drawer and read them to me, widening her eyes over the parts about how Mom had neglected to pick her up from school when Nancy was sick with bronchitis, and about how trash and dirt piled up in the room they shared. At the time, no one I knew questioned that childcare and cleaning were primarily the wife's responsibilities, even if she had a demanding job and a higher salary than her husband—as Mom did during the first decade of my life. My father accused her of having a love affair with her boss, and with one of the gardeners on the organic farm where she volunteered on Saturdays. She saved up money to move out, and we all continued to live in the house while my parents argued over custody of Nancy and me.

.

One afternoon, my father put Mom's tarot cards in the trash, saying they were "of the devil," and threw her brightly colored paisley
dresses, hippie blouses, and mandala-patterned pants on the lawn.
Nancy held me while Mom picked up the clothes, packed her car,
and said she'd come back for us. She rented an apartment on the
outskirts of Chadds Ford and asked Nancy and me how we'd feel
about bunk beds. For the next year and a half, we spent weekend
nights at Mom's, where Nancy, maybe just to scare me, kept a knife
under her mattress.

.

My mother was a political activist and an environmentalist; this,
combined with her mania, got her fired from DuPont. During a
lunch break, she told her colleagues that DuPont illegally dumped
chemicals in the Chesapeake Bay, poisoning waterbirds and other
wildlife, and that they all should organize a protest. Security guards
escorted her from the building. Later on, she said she was happy
to have lost that job. The most important thing in life, she told my
sister and me, was to find something we liked doing, and never to
work anywhere too long just for money.

A headhunter found her a systems analysis job in Huntsville,
Alabama, and she surprised my family by taking it. If she liked it,
she said, she'd find a way for my sister and me to move down there
with her. My father said there was no way that was happening; he
believed that Mom was still in the throes of the manic episode that
had gotten her fired and that we had to let it run its course. She

got rid of the white Volkswagen bug I loved, leased a brand-new sports car, a Chrysler Conquest, and was gone. I was embarrassed to tell my friends, whose mothers stayed at home, that Mom had left our family. I counted the days until Nancy and I were to visit her down South.

•

In 1986, when I was seven, I took my first plane ride, with Nancy, to visit Mom in her new place in Alabama. Nancy stared straight ahead during takeoff and landing, so I knew she was scared, too.

We found Mom waiting for us at the airport, wearing bright red lipstick, dangly clip-on earrings, and a long sleeveless dress with a zebra print. She hugged us both and packed us into the Conquest to show us around Huntsville. It was hot, and the city air was humid and polluted. I wondered where the trees were. But Mom's condo was cool and full of plants and new, modern furniture, including a fancy stereo. She put on Gordon Lightfoot's "Sundown" and danced around her new digs, snapping her fingers. I thought that Mom must be making a lot of money. That night, she took us to see *Crocodile Dundee* and let Nancy and me drink all the Coke we wanted.

Before we left, Mom asked us if we wanted to come back to Alabama and live with her. We both said yes.

•

After several months in Huntsville, Mom had fulfilled her temporary contract but wasn't offered a permanent job. She returned to

Chadds Ford with her once-long hair in a short, frizzy perm; I was relieved that she'd made some kind of arrangement with my father and was moving back home. She found a part-time job teaching technical writing at a community college, gave it up after a year or two, and afterward relied on my father to support our family. He didn't complain. After all, he'd won, and he seemed to enjoy the role of provider, as long as his wife and children behaved the way he thought we should.

Back at home, Mom kept Nancy and me at arm's length while she took exhaustive notes on the novels, plays, and history and pop science books that she brought home in piles from the library. I was afraid that her independent mind would prompt her to leave us again. But I came to understand that even if she wanted to, she didn't have the energy anymore.

.

Our family was essentially isolated. My parents seldom socialized and had no friends they saw regularly. My father, Nancy, and I spent Thanksgivings visiting his brother and his family in New Jersey. My mother preferred to stay home; she believed that the Europeans' arrival in America, and their subsequent domination of Native Americans, was nothing to celebrate.

I did go to see my grandmother and my mother's sister, Tina, in Coatesville and Lancaster, respectively. But my cousin Elizabeth, who was the daughter of my mother's and Tina's brother Sam, and a year older than me, was born in the Philippines, and since my family didn't travel much—and certainly not overseas—I didn't really know her as a child. She was taller than Nancy and me, and we grew up wearing her hand-me-downs. When her family moved back to the States, they lived in Westport, Connecticut, and then moved to Seattle.

In the early 1990s, a few years after Mom was home from Alabama, my father accepted a buyout from DuPont that included a decent pension, and he became a stockbroker. He got an entry-level job at Shearson Lehman Hutton, which became Shearson Lehman Brothers and then Smith Barney. After that, we rarely saw him: he worked long hours and sometimes had to spend time in New York. On Christmas mornings, he left packages addressed to Mom, Nancy, and me on the kitchen table before heading to church. After a year or two, we knew their contents without opening them: there'd be three nearly identical sweaters in different colors, and three identical gold necklaces, each with a tiny pearl, gift-wrapped by a clerk. Over the winter, Mom and I would share and trade all three sweaters. Nancy never wore those things our father gave her.

8.

By the summer of 1997, when I was eighteen, James and I had broken up—he was still in high school when I went to college—and Atlantis planned a cross-country road trip that was supposed to be just us girls. It would take two weeks and would cost each of us $500 to share cheap motel rooms and discover America. At the last minute, she invited our mother, who said she'd love to come along.

Since three people wouldn't fit in the Alfa, we took Mom's Honda Accord, which she had special-ordered without AC to save the earth. We headed west on the Dreamway, a nickname for the Pennsylvania Turnpike, America's first limited-access divided highway.

Mom and Atlantis both loved to drive, and we all preferred wind and blaring music to conversation. Despite the billboards advertising natural wonders and historical sites, we seldom took an exit. Mom played cassette tapes—Fleetwood Mac, Tracy Chapman, Eurythmics. Atlantis ashed her cigarettes out the window.

She told us her own songs were written for the girls who spent their lives trapped in the Middle West behind cash registers. We all got excited whenever we crossed another state line. Every time we stopped for gas, Atlantis headed for the postcard displays. She bought the silliest ones and mailed them to her old friends, and her crushes, back in Pennsylvania. At night, she and Mom shared a bed and stayed up talking as I drifted in and out of sleep. Once, at a Super 8 in New Mexico, I overheard Atlantis asking Mom about her suicide attempt. Had she been pissed when she woke up in the hospital bed?

"Well, frankly, yes," Mom said. "But don't you girls ever try anything like that. You may live to regret it."

"Can you please talk about something else?" I said from my side of the room. "Or tell better stories?"

"You're lucky not to know what it feels like to want to die," Atlantis said. "Our stories suck because our lives have sucked."

"You *are* lucky, Betsy," Mom said.

"Yeah, I hit the jackpot with you two," I said.

"Lucky Betsy," Atlantis said, coining a new nickname. "Mom! Tell us about the time that lunatic asshole held you at gunpoint and ejaculated all over you."

"It was in Seattle in 1973," Mom began. "I was coming home after a cello concert . . ."

I'd heard this story before. In fact, I'd written about it in an essay for a high school English class. Mom had been fishing keys from her purse when she was accosted by a middle-aged man saying, "See this gun, baby? Open the fuckin' door." She was thirty. The man forced Mom into the basement of a house that she rented alone, yanked up her skirt, came on her, and fled. She filed a police report, but they never found the man. It wasn't rape, Mom explained, because there had been no penetration. After the assault, she submitted her dissertation, "Communicatory Accuracy in Four Experiments," got her PhD and a teaching job in Wisconsin. Her first nervous breakdown took place within a year. She recovered on her stepfather's hundred-plus-acre sheep farm on Gum Tree Road in Coatesville, Pennsylvania. Then she went to work at DuPont and met my father, the most reliable man she'd ever known.

.

In 1998, Atlantis transferred her Loyola credits to Penn State, moved into an apartment in State College, and tried to kill herself by taking pills and drinking. Before she passed out, she stumbled around her apartment and knocked over a table. A neighbor heard the noise and called the police. Atlantis was hospitalized, then took the rest of the semester off and moved back home with Mom and Dad again.

I was in England, on a junior-year-abroad program at Oxford, studying poetry, when I heard about it. On the phone, Atlantis told me she was back on antidepressants, and that Penn State was obsessed with football culture. The few gay people there had to stay in the closet or get raped, she said, and the winter was enough to make you slit your wrists.

She was still in Chadds Ford two months later, when my father fell down at work and was diagnosed with a brain tumor. Doctors said that if he chose chemotherapy, he might have several more years to live—perhaps a decade. When he began treatments, I was still at Oxford, and everyone in my family agreed that I should remain abroad, and that Atlantis and Mom would take care of him.

.

My father had the first real leisure time in his life while he battled his illness. His months were taken up with books my mother gave him. He also read my copy of *Animal Liberation*, and I was stunned when he sent me a note saying that it had taught him something. He wasn't going to become a vegetarian, he wrote, but his doctors had taken him off red meat, and he really couldn't disagree with Singer that it was unnecessary to kill animals.

When I got back from Oxford, he was in the intensive care wing at a hospital on the main line outside of Philadelphia. Atlantis, meanwhile, had crashed the Alfa and gotten a DUI and was spending two months in rehab at White Deer Run in lieu of a thirty-day jail sentence.

My father's cancer treatments hadn't worked the way the doctors had hoped. During the last three weeks of his life, I spent most of the time just sitting with him as he dozed, high on morphine. I remembered how he'd planted most of the trees in our yard and taught me their names: dogwood, birch, Japanese weeping cherry, burning bush. His devotion to traditional ideas of marriage must have saved our family when Mom was too sick to care for anyone, especially herself. If he hadn't believed that being a father, husband, and provider were lifelong duties, what might have happened to my mother, sister, and me? As I sat there watching him, I couldn't forget his bouts of violence, but I knew that I took after him in one essential way. I was committed to loving the people in my family, not because they were easy or even kind, but because they had been given to me.

Once, he woke up and reached for me. He touched my hair— lightly, lovingly. My father.

·

So that she could go to our father's funeral, Atlantis was given a reprieve of several hours from her rehab facility. She walked into St. Cornelius Church wearing red lipstick, a short black dress, and stockings, and squeezed into a pew between me and Mom. Had she borrowed this getup from someone at the facility? Neither of us had been back to church since we'd been confirmed Angela (her) and Theresa (me). After Christ Church Cathedral and the Bodleian Library—sights that had become commonplace for me over the last ten months—St. Cornelius felt small and provincial. Atlantis jabbed me, and I followed her eyes to see Mrs. Smith, a severe-looking woman in the front pew.

Mrs. Smith was the mother of five children, all girls, with their hair pulled into ponytails tight enough to make their eyes slant; she was the strictest of all the parents I knew at our church. Heather, one of the Smith girls, was my best childhood friend. Once, when I was six, I saw Mrs. Smith beating Heather's bare bottom with a wooden spoon, and when she caught me watching, she ordered me to go away unless I wanted a turn.

After the ceremony, Mrs. Smith came up to me. "Your father was a good man," she said.

In the receiving line, I spotted Father Walker speaking to my mother. I couldn't believe he was still alive. He'd officiated at my parents' wedding and baptized both Atlantis and me. My sister and I had spent countless Saturday evenings talking in low voices to this man whose face was a shadow behind a screen; our father had met with him face-to-face. I linked arms with Atlantis and went out to the parking lot without a word to Father Walker.

An attendant stood waiting by a white van to take Atlantis back to rehab. Our father would be buried in New Jersey, next to his sister, in a plot that his parents had purchased when he was a year old. But his firstborn wasn't allowed to cross state lines, so I would be the daughter to witness his body being laid to rest.

In San Francisco, I opened for Johnette Napolitano from Concrete Blonde. It was the biggest performance I'd ever done in my life. And it was the first sober performance I'd ever done in my life. I had a drummer and Andrew, my West Coast guitar player, play with me. Johnette was just doing acoustic, so they didn't want the whole band there. To put an acoustic guitar in front of you in your lap, it's one step away from being stripped down naked. She was such a real person. And, uh, I like the fact that she made a comeback. Because that sort of inspires me, being that I'm thirty-one and I'm like, am I too old to be doing this as a woman? I'm like, well hell. If Johnette's kickin' it up there, why can't I?

9.

With my father gone, Mom was rich, thanks to his life insurance policy, and she wanted to travel with Atlantis and me. She took us on a vacation to Hawaii; I lost track of how many beers Atlantis drank on the plane. She and Mom spent most of their time sunbathing on the hotel balcony while I went hiking in the rain forest. Nights I swam alone in the wonderfully warm water; Atlantis stayed out late at gay bars and Mom lounged in an armchair in the room the three of us shared, reading mystery novels.

.

I was accepted to Columbia University's graduate creative writing program in poetry at the same time that Atlantis got her bachelor's degree from Penn State, in geographic information systems. She'd chosen the field of cartography because she loved maps and had heard it paid decently. She got a job as a technician for the New York State Task Force on Demographic Research and Reapportionment in Manhattan and asked me to rent an apartment with her. Since she'd destroyed her credit in Los Angeles, I was hesitant to do it. But she had a salary, and I had student loans. She also had a truck—a Toyota Tacoma that Mom had helped her to buy, after the Alfa wasn't salvageable—and she offered to help me move. We found another roommate and a rat- and roach-infested sixth-floor walk-up on West 122nd Street. She took the smallest bedroom in order to pay less in rent and kept fiendish track of our expenses. She played open-mic nights at the SideWalk Café on East Sixth Street and Avenue A and invited me to come along, and we began to have some of the same friends. She spent most of her money on rehearsal space for the band she was forming with Ray, a woman in her late thirties who played bass and who became her lover.

Her shows got louder and more punk. I brought friends along, and she recruited my new boyfriend, Kyle, as her drummer. She would call me onstage, where I shook a tambourine and sang backup as she growled and screamed. Once, when she lost a pick, she played her fingers raw and spattered her guitar with blood.

·

On September 10, 2001, at about 7:00 p.m., I stopped by Atlantis's office at 250 Broadway; we went out, danced, and got drunk at a Schwervon! show. I didn't try to conceal my annoyance when she changed plans and decided to go home early to Ray's place in Brooklyn instead of riding back to Morningside Heights with me. The next morning, I was awakened by a message being left on the answering machine I shared with Atlantis. It was one of her colleagues at the task force.

"Atlantis, I don't know what time you're planning to come in, but if you haven't left already, please don't come to work today. Something happened to the World Trade Center. We're being evacuated . . . there are fireballs . . . I got to go."

I tried to call Atlantis's cell phone. No answer. I managed to reach my mother in Ephrata, Pennsylvania, where she'd moved after my father died. She hadn't heard from Atlantis either.

Hours passed before I was able to talk to her. She'd been getting ready to leave for work when the first tower was hit, and she and Ray had been sitting on the roof in the South Slope all day, drinking beer and watching the smoke. When her office reopened, she and her coworkers were required to participate in private therapy sessions with a psychiatrist. The doctor assigned to Atlantis asked if the attacks had traumatized her. She said yes and got him to prescribe Valium.

·

Atlantis built a website in the early 2000s, before most unsigned musicians had one. On it, she described herself as "a depressed girl who can't sing and doesn't give a fuck." She asked a photographer friend named Orianna to do a shoot for her first album, *In My Bed*, whose songs were about love, depression, and suicide. Orianna took pictures of Atlantis on the roof of our Morningside Heights apartment. While Atlantis was writing material for her second album, *More than Opium*, she again asked Orianna for help. These songs were about surviving sexual abuse, addiction, and trying to get clean. The concept of the shoot seemed on the nose: a young woman returns to the hometown she had hated as a teenager.

So Orianna joined Atlantis for an overnight trip to Chadds Ford. Years later, I asked Orianna what that trip was like. She said that Atlantis already seemed to be on drugs in the morning when they met at the car rental place, and she saw her taking more pills on the drive down. Atlantis told her that she felt comfortable taking off her clothes for Orianna to take pictures of her, but that was it—they couldn't have sex. Had Atlantis forgotten that Orianna was straight and happily married to her high school sweetheart? And did she realize she could make art with someone without that person having other expectations? Orianna let her know she was simply there to do her job.

The outdoor, daytime photographs made me nostalgic: Atlantis sitting on the trestle in the woods, looking vulnerable and lovable. Then they checked into the Holiday Inn, where Atlantis took off most of her clothes, flipped on the TV, and started drinking.

"How do you want to look?" Orianna asked.

Atlantis said: "Make me look desperate."

·

One Christmas Eve, when we were both in our twenties and visiting Mom in Ephrata, I thought I must have been hallucinating when I saw Atlantis preparing something in the kitchen—my sister found food boring and had never bothered to learn how to cook. Also, there was no stove. When Mom moved into her house and found that the previous owners had taken it with them, she refused to replace it. She told me she had no use for a stove, since she already had a toaster oven, and she'd found a hot plate at Goodwill. She'd rolled a metal cart next to the refrigerator, where the stove had been, and put her toaster oven on it, and the hot plate on top of that.

Atlantis was standing over the hot plate, stirring a pot of brown liquid. She said it was opium tea, brewed from dried poppies she'd ordered on the internet from Afghanistan. She offered steaming mugs to Mom and me and told us to ignore the foul taste. Mom declined; I accepted. The taste wasn't that bad. Atlantis got out her guitar and asked me to accompany her on the piano. My spinet hadn't been tuned in a while, but I'd lost my usual self-consciousness. Mom wandered into the living room and sat down to listen; the next morning, she asked if we planned to record our "miraculous" songs.

·

In 2002, I got my MFA from Columbia and was offered a job as assistant to the director at the 92Y's Unterberg Poetry Center. The not-for-profit administrative world demanded many overtime hours—a couple of nights a week for readings and events, and some weekends to support the writing program and the literary brunches. The position paid little, but it would connect me to hundreds of writers and people in the publishing industry, give me a library of free books, and enable me to live in New York City without scrounging for adjunct teaching positions or competitive freelance writing gigs. After three years, I was promoted to managing director, and then, the following year, to acting director. A year after that, I was director. This exhilarating, exhausting job became my life. It left me little time to read, do my own writing, or have a serious romantic relationship, but I believed that all that would come later.

Mom came to New York for events I hosted at the 92Y but was always too shy to speak to the writers she so admired and whose work she'd introduced me to—John Updike, Günter Grass, E. L. Doctorow, A. S. Byatt. Still, I was proud to have been able to bring her to breathe the same air as her literary heroes. Atlantis joined Mom and me for one 92Y reading by Margaret Atwood. My sister had read *Cat's Eye*, *The Handmaid's Tale*, and a collection called *Murder in the Dark*.

In the summer of 2006, seven years after my father died, Mom called out of the blue and said she'd paid off my student loans. She'd written a five-digit check to Sallie Mae.

·

Atlantis spent five years in New York City, playing shows and supporting herself with her government job. After she and Ray broke up, she went on Nerve.com and fell for a woman calling herself luvmedo, who turned out to be Leah, a sweet, beautiful hip-hop DJ who was about Atlantis's age, and just coming out as a lesbian. They met for drinks, hit it off, and luvmedo accepted that Atlantis didn't listen to the Beatles. Atlantis moved into Leah's one-bedroom apartment in Hell's Kitchen; their domestic bliss was the subject of a photo spread in *Metro New York*. When Leah got a job offer to do hip-hop programming at MTV in San Francisco, she invited Atlantis to move with her. Atlantis played a farewell show at Arlene's Grocery and headed west.

TWO

10.

By 2007—the year before Atlantis disappeared—I had lived in New York City for seven years. Then I was offered a job teaching poetry for two semesters on the Greek island of Paros: I would have little cell phone or internet access, and a year to focus on writing. I got a sabbatical from the Y, gave up my apartment, and stored my things.

I assume that Atlantis was already addicted to painkillers when she enrolled in a program to become a pharmacy technician in San Francisco; she called the band she formed there Drugstore Cowgirl. Though I was skeptical about her career plan, Atlantis said that given her psychopharmacological experience, she already knew everything that she could be tested on. I couldn't really argue with her: after years of Paxil for depression, Depakote (prescribed in the early 2000s) to prevent seizures, and benzos for panic attacks, Atlantis was an expert.

.

That summer, I got a call from Leah: Atlantis had nearly died after supposedly swallowing a bottle of Xanax over the course of a night. I had a month before my job in Greece began, and flew out to California. I took my sister hiking in Yosemite, and the short, steep walk to the top of Glacier Point was too much for her. One minute she was gazing down at the treetops below; the next, she was seizing, her lips turning blue. A stranger put a leather boot in her mouth before two hikers, who happened to be doctors, intervened.

That night in our hotel room, Atlantis put down her copy of *Anna Karenina* and confided to me that her depression had gotten worse since she'd moved west. She wasn't writing songs, she hadn't made friends, and she and Leah were in couples therapy. She admitted that what she'd taken wasn't Xanax but morphine; she'd hoped to die in the comfort of Leah's arms.

This was the third time I was aware of that Atlantis had tried to kill herself. She was welcome to visit me in Greece, I told her— seeing ancient temples, or just sitting in the strong sunlight, would lift anyone's depression. She said she didn't have the money or the energy to travel and told me not to mind if she died. I *did* mind, I said, and I would never give her permission to hurt herself; if she couldn't travel to Greece, I'd definitely visit her when I got back. I hoped that meanwhile she'd go to a hospital and get some real help.

I don't know exactly how Atlantis first got into prescription painkillers, but certainly various doctors had prescribed her hydrocodone or codeine when she had whiplash or needed dental work. When she couldn't get it from her doctors regularly, or when she ran out, she went on the internet and ordered it from a pharmacy in the Philippines that would mail it to her. Was that also where she'd gotten the morphine?

·

A week before I left, a former teacher told me a disturbing story about the school where I was scheduled to teach. Years ago, she said, a group of men on the island had gang-raped a local woman, and one of the heads of the school had filmed it. She never saw the film, but her husband had witnessed the crime and told her about it. The rape was never reported to the police, and the fact that her husband had been among those who failed to intervene or report it led to a fight that ultimately ended my teacher's marriage. I thanked her for telling me and said that I would be vigilant.

·

Paros is thirteen miles long and ten miles wide, a landscape both easy to navigate and easy to lose your way in. Near the coast, I could orient myself by the position of the sun, the bay, the mountain, and the lighthouse. Often, though, I got lost on the winding, unmarked roads in the interior, where stone walls divided the rocky farms. Paros had one small forest left, near the ferry port; most of the pines had been cut down long ago to build boats, but some olive and cypress trees were said to be two thousand years old.

The white stucco house I lived in was a couple of miles above the town, halfway up a mountain. It had one story, deep-set windows, and an arch-shaped wooden door. My favorite part of the house was the back patio, with reclining chairs, a marble table, gardens, and a view of the Aegean. Stray cats sunned on the stone terrace while I worked. One fat orange tomcat liked to pad over the pages of the science fiction novel I was writing. When he sprawled across my notebook, I knew it was time to put down my pen and scratch his belly.

I wore my mother's straw hat and rode a bicycle to the class I taught two days a week. And I found a friend and lover in Dan, a painting teacher from Toronto. We made excursions to the mountain village of Lefkes, to clay beaches, to the fishing village of Aliki. We spent our days writing and painting, hiking and swimming, and our nights in tavernas, eating, drinking, and dancing.

Atlantis and my mother would have liked that place.

.

Just before Atlantis's thirty-first birthday (we were both Scorpios, four days apart), Dan and I guided a group of students through Selçuk, Turkey, to the ancient city of Ephesus. Somewhere near the "House of the Virgin Mary"—where the Holy Mother is said to have died—a woman was selling jewelry. Her long, dark hair reminded me of Atlantis's. I picked up one of the pendants from her table: it was a small, silver sun, with thirteen tiny eyes at the flame tips. The woman said the necklace was extremely powerful and would ward off bad spirits; I told her that my sister in California would love it. The woman said my sister probably needed protection—she could feel something—and what a good sister I was to be thinking of her halfway around the world. She dangled it on a simple black cord, and the sun flashed in all those evil eyes. The necklace cost the equivalent of a hundred dollars—more than I could afford—but I was inexperienced at haggling and the woman knew I wanted it. Also, she frightened me. I paid what she asked and mailed the pendant to San Francisco.

A week later, I heard from Atlantis:

THANK YOU SISTER!!!!! It is gorgeous and I adore the "spell quality" to it—it means the world to me.

.

The next time I spoke with Atlantis, she said that she and Leah had agreed to start living separately at the end of the year. She'd have her pharmacy tech degree by then, and she planned to move to San Diego. I advised her to move back to the East Coast, where she actually knew people, but she said that she couldn't stand another New York winter. I told her that teaching on Paros was sketchy, and Dan wasn't able to make plans with me. I wanted to come back to the States. Could I help her with the move? No, she said, she needed every inch of space in her truck, but why didn't I return home and visit Mom, who wanted to see me.

.

One afternoon in December, Atlantis called me in Greece, sounding terrified. "Something bad happened," she said. "I need you to do something for me. Get a pen."

A sting operation had gone down, she said, in the San Francisco hospital where she worked as a pharmacy intern. Two men from the FBI had interviewed her and her colleagues, and she thought one of the men was now stalking her.

I told her to calm down. Probably someone she worked with had made a mistake, and the authorities were just trying to get to the bottom of it. Had she taken any drugs from the hospital? No, she said, but false arrests were common for people with jobs like hers. Was she still seeing her psychotherapist? No, she couldn't afford it anymore; she was just visiting a psychiatrist from time to time to get her medications.

She asked me to come up with a date and place where we could meet in a worst-case scenario. It had to be in a foreign country. Delusional as she might have been, Atlantis's pain was real, and I knew she wasn't kidding about going into hiding, even if no one was looking for her. But at least she was talking about living instead of dying. I told her that if anything ever happened that forced either of us to disappear, we could meet in front of the *Mona Lisa* at high noon on the Fourth of July, any year. Perfect, she said.

.

On my way out of America, at a friend's suggestion, I'd signed up for Facebook and invited Atlantis to join. The next time I opened Atlantis's Facebook page, I noticed that she was friends with someone I will refer to as Gretchen. At the time, I wondered who she was—and now that I know more about her, it's clear to me that I can't use her real name.

.

Over Christmas, I visited Mom and presented her with an icon from the House of the Virgin Mary in Turkey.

"Oh," she said, "you're so sentimental. No, that's not the word I want. Betsy, you're so weird."

I said that primitive art was always sentimental and weird, and if she didn't like it, I would give it to someone who did.

"It's funny how different you are from your sister," she said. "Atlantis is virtually un-insultable. I call her a functioning drug addict and she doesn't even blink. You've always been so sensitive."

I told her that Atlantis was barely functioning, and that we didn't have to have a relationship if she didn't want one.

"I'm a blunt person," she said. "It's hard to say anything at all to someone so sensitive, sticking out all over the place."

Later that evening, Mom slipped a peace offering under my door: a business reply envelope from *Wired* magazine, on the back of which she'd written: "'Lost & found' words for Betsy: imaginative, romantic, wonderful (adj. weird and w.), loving, agapistic, demonstrative."

.

In January, Atlantis changed her status on Facebook from being in a relationship to being single, and the city where she lived from San Francisco to San Diego. She sent me a few group emails that included Gretchen and someone named Psychobunny as their recipients. I didn't pay much attention to the emails. One was a photograph of Christina Ricci from the movie *Monster*, in which she plays a teenage girl who gets picked up by Aileen Wuornos, the serial killer and former prostitute. Atlantis joked that she'd gotten a bad haircut and now looked just like her.

.

Dan called from Toronto—he'd also gone home for the holidays—
and asked if we might spend some time together in New York City
on his way back to Athens. After seeing him again, I decided
to find a way to return to Greece. Neither of us was going back
to the school where we'd been teaching, and I had a full semester without plans. I hoped to live somewhere inexpensively and
work on my novel. I found an artist residency through the Aegean
Center for the Fine Arts and signed up for Greek language classes
in Athens. I shared my good news with Atlantis; she wrote back
immediately:

> *I am SO proud of you, Sister :)*

> *I really want to write a book too—but I have no idea what
> it would be about or where to begin. I suppose with a plot
> outline—but as much as people have urged me to, I could
> NEVER write an autobiography—perhaps I'll leave that up to
> you, E. Bronte :)*

> *Yes, we Must talk. Call me soon.*

> *XOXO*
> *—the Other Bronte*

.

While I was in New York, I heard about a job opening at the
Pierrepont School, a progressive k–12 private school in Westport,
Connecticut. I knew I didn't want to return to arts administration

in the fall. During my semester in Greece, I'd decided that teaching was my vocation. I needed more legitimate teaching experience, ideally in a place where I might lure Dan to join me. I interviewed and was hired. In the fall, I would be teaching English four days a week to students aged seven to seventeen, and an after-school creative writing class. My students would be bright and motivated, and each class would be capped at twelve. I asked if they also needed a painting teacher. It was possible, they said.

.

After the holidays, Mom visited San Diego, where she stayed with an old friend from college. She and Atlantis apparently had a great time together, and Mom made an impulsive decision to resettle there if she could sell her house; she returned to Ephrata and put her house on the market. Atlantis warned her that San Diego was expensive, but she fully supported Mom's moving there and sent her listings for bungalows and condos.

.

On February 20, I received a copy of an email from Atlantis that was addressed to Kyle, my ex-boyfriend who'd played in her band:

Hi K—

I'm making this a mass email so I don't have to tell the story a thousand times. I got the job but then *didn't* get the job when they looked back on my blackout dates and saw that I would be

unable to work from March 13th-17th (I have a friend coming
into town and we've been planning on this for MONTHS—she
already bought her ticket and has never been to SD and knows
no one here and we were planning to go to Mexico together).

I found it irritating that my sister appeared to have remained so close
with my ex. The story didn't sound like much, and I wasn't sure why
she was telling it to a group. What job was she trying to get? After
the FBI sting at the San Francisco hospital, I thought Atlantis was
afraid to—or couldn't—work in pharmacy, and she was looking for
any old job to pay the rent. I didn't know who the mysterious friend
was. I wrote back and asked her who, but she didn't reply.

·

In March, she sent a mass email with the subject "Trailer for the
film I'm in," along with a video link to the trailer of a movie adapta-
tion of Shakespeare's *As You Like It*, directed by Pete Shaner. Later
that month, I finally got an email from her:

So right now I have an editing job for University Readers—
it's only PT and my hours suck and the pay sucks even worse—
but at least it's something. That's why I've gotten into modeling
and acting. I'm in a Samuel L. Jackson film next month, as
well as a Matthew McConaughey and Ashton Kutcher movie.
Nothing big—just bit-roles and extra parts. But at least they
feed me and give me $150 a pop. I feel sick over the whole thing
because I am not, and never wanted to be, an actress. I feel that
I'm taking away chances from 19-year-old girls from Nebraska

who were molested and saved every dime from their cashier
jobs just to get to CA and their dream is to be an actress.

I didn't believe all this. When she was in her twenties, people who
saw her on the street used to offer her modeling gigs. But movies
with Samuel L. Jackson and Matthew McConaughey? I wondered
what she was really doing. Her email continued:

Gretchen flew in from NYC the other week to film a
documentary on me—but after seeing the footage I do not
ever want it to be released. She and her editor are determined
however—so it's a battle.

So that was the mysterious friend. When we talked on the phone
and I asked Atlantis who Gretchen was, she acted as if she'd already
told me about her. Atlantis said that Gretchen was a fan who'd been
especially interested in her experience as a female rocker. They'd
been internet friends for about a year. When Gretchen asked if
they could meet in person, Atlantis, who answered all of her fan
mail, said she was moving from San Francisco to San Diego, and
that Gretchen could come and shoot whenever she wanted.

I wasn't sure what Atlantis believed about Gretchen. It wasn't a
romance, Atlantis said. She wasn't physically attracted to Gretchen,
and their relationship involved no sex.

From my first record, the last song, "My Machine," it's all about my vibrator. Every girl I've been with says, "I want to make you come without that stupid vibrator!" I have never come with another human being. I can only come with my vibrator. I can get people off in my sleep. It's just sort of a curse I was born with. You know?

11.

In April, Atlantis emailed me again. She'd found a great job with the California League of Conservation Voters. And she'd begun writing a short autobiographical piece that recounted her departure from New York City for California after a bad experience with a psychotherapist. She said that the story would be about her "mental breakdown" and "subsequent spiral into drugs and alcohol," and asked me if I'd read the first couple of pages, since I was "the writer" in the family.

I was well aware of Atlantis's hostility to her former psychotherapist—who seemed to have dumped her—but I hadn't realized that she thought she'd had a "breakdown" as a result of their falling-out. Sure, I said, send the pages.

Atlantis's untitled memoir began: "It was a profoundly terrible bliss . . ."

I wrote back some encouraging words. I advised her to keep going, and not to get too caught up with trying to make her language sound poetic. "In this case," I wrote, "the facts may be poetry enough." She thought that was hilarious.

ATLANTIS'S FACEBOOK UPDATES

April 17

Atlantis is mainlining.

Atlantis is calling poison control because she just realized that what she thought what [sic] China White was actually Anthrax.

.

A Facebook friend messaged her with the subject "as if": "there is ANY China White on the West coast. Not that I would know anything about that." She messaged him back: "Oh honey, I run a whole cartel from Barstow to Bejing [*sic*] . . ."

She was obviously kidding, pretending to be some big-time drug dealer. Atlantis couldn't afford the rent for her shared apartment.

.

The next time we spoke on the phone, she told me that she was involved in a class-action lawsuit against a company called Avidhosting. com, which provided website domains. Atlantis had used their service, and her website had frozen without warning or explanation. The suit seemed legitimate: the same thing had happened to hundreds of other Avidhosting patrons, who continued to be charged monthly fees for domains to which they no longer had access. Artists and entrepreneurs lost thousands of dollars. Rumors circulated that the owner had died, and that the new owner was selling Avidhosting members' domain names to people who appeared to be hackers. Eventually, patrons received a mass email saying they could get their domain names back if they sent fifteen dollars to an address in Texas. Atlantis got in touch with other victims, collected names, and emailed the FBI to report the scam.

On April 20, Atlantis received an email from someone asking if she was organizing the Avidhosting lawsuit and, if so, whether she had any help. She responded that she was doing it on her own and called herself "the Erin Brockovich of cyberspace."

The next morning, a pair of agents from the Drug Enforcement Agency woke her up at the apartment she was subletting in San Diego. (Later, she claimed they'd broken down her door.) The agents questioned her about a Vicodin purchase at a Target pharmacy in San Diego the month before. Atlantis said she believed that someone—she didn't say who—was using her ID to get prescriptions, and that she'd told both the pharmacist and her doctor about it. She said that she'd had the pharmacist photocopy her driver's license so that no one else could get her prescriptions.

I knew better than to believe everything I read in Atlantis's emails, but these details also appear in the Department of Justice's investigative report.

The agent asked Atlantis if she'd given her credit card to anyone. She said no, but then added, "Well, maybe if I'm in the car waiting." She denied doing anything wrong, and said she'd been prescribed Vicodin after a car accident. She'd been taking it for months, she said, and it made her memory "a little fuzzy."

Why had she gone to Target to pick up the prescription after trying to get it at Walgreens? She used both pharmacies, she said, and couldn't remember which one had called her saying that her prescription was ready. When it wasn't at Walgreens, she'd assumed it was at Target.

The agent said that Target didn't have an automated telephone calling system for controlled substances. Atlantis told him she used to work at Walgreens—which the agents already knew—and that such a system had been in place there. Finally she said, "If you have to arrest me, go ahead."

The agents cuffed her, still in her pajamas, confiscated her cell phone, and took her to Las Colinas, a jail in Santee, a suburb of San Diego. Had her identity been stolen or had she given it away and let herself be used? In either case, I thought it was strange that she'd been arrested so soon after reaching out to the FBI about Avidhosting.com. But it might have just been a coincidence; after all, the DEA isn't the FBI.

12.

I was riding on the back of a friend's motorcycle, visiting Naxos for the first time, on the day Atlantis was arrested; I was island-hopping during the week she spent in jail. Nobody in my family told me what had happened.

Atlantis's San Diego roommate emailed my aunt Tina (our mother's sister) from Atlantis's account; he said that Atlantis had been arrested and needed help. When a bail bondsman phoned Mom, she assumed he was a con artist. And when she learned that Atlantis really had been arrested on charges of burglary and pre-scription drug fraud, and required $1,000 for a $10,000 bond, she told my aunt that she'd decided not to give her any more "hand-outs." She told the bondsman's supervisor, to get it on record, that her daughter was a drug addict and a "flight risk."

Mom kept all this a secret from me and forbade my aunt to tell me. But my aunt thought I should know and emailed me about it. Mom was being cheap; but she trusted that the system worked, and that authorities would figure out that Atlantis needed medical attention. By the time I heard what had happened, Atlantis had spent six days in jail. I sent her an email at the detention center the same day she'd finally managed to bail herself out with a credit card.

.

She emailed me a photograph of bruises on her arms and legs, with a message that began:

> *I am out.*
> *Email is not safe.*
> *Nor are phone calls.*
> *I am writing our mother out of my life . . .*

Deprived of her medications, including the antiseizure drug she took daily, Atlantis had had a grand mal seizure in the courtroom, delaying her arraignment. She'd also gone on a hunger strike in jail and said that the guards had "pushed her around" when she refused to eat.

> *And that is nothing—many girls were whisked off to isolation with broken arms.*

> *I've done a lot of things in my life—but of these charges I am 100% innocent. I am getting a top-notch attorney and am not only pleading not guilty but am counter-suing for false-arrest, abuse and medical neglect while incarcerated.*

*All in all, there is no evidence, no proof, nothing. The law firm
has a steadfast reputation to protect—therefore they do not take
on cases they believe they can't win—and according to them,
mine is a "slam dunk."*

If she pleaded guilty, Atlantis would get a mandatory eighteen-month
sentence, and there was no guarantee that she would be able to serve it
in rehab. She decided to fight the charges. She claimed to me that she
wasn't stressed about any of this, and she employed our code word: "I
turn my mind to the beautiful artistry of the Mona Lisa."

She was referring to our agreement to meet at the Louvre
should she ever decide to run away for good. She closed her email
saying she'd get a calling card and try me from a pay phone. .

.

Atlantis used to say that we both "drew aces in the looks and intelli-
gence departments," but that somehow I'd been blessed with a dis-
proportionate share of luck. When we were children, Atlantis had
protected me from all manner of harm—when she herself wasn't
trying to kill me. But our relationship wasn't about my paying off
some impossible debt. I loved my sister, however troubled and trou-
bling she was.

.

The prescription purchase that got Atlantis arrested took place
around the same time Gretchen visited San Diego to shoot video
of Atlantis.

Here's what I found out: On March 19, someone claiming to be a nurse practitioner had called in a Vicodin prescription under my sister's name. The pharmacist who'd received the call-in found the order suspicious—it was for a higher dosage than Atlantis had had before and included the instruction to "take as needed." The pharmacist called the nurse practitioner's office; they said the prescription was fraudulent and told the pharmacist to obtain a copy of the driver's license of anyone who tried to pick it up.

Atlantis visited Walgreens that evening and told the pharmacist who waited on her that she'd received a "weird call" from her doctor's office about her Vicodin prescription. Atlantis commented that someone was trying to use her identification. The pharmacist said Walgreens needed a copy of her license to maintain on file. The Department of Justice's report goes on to say that while Atlantis was standing at the pickup counter, someone impersonating the nurse practitioner left a new voicemail amending the fraudulent prescription. Atlantis stood waiting while the pharmacist said that the prescription had to be confirmed. Then she said there was a problem and suggested that Atlantis come back the next day. My sister left empty-handed.

An hour later, a woman who the DEA report says fit the description of Atlantis—but whom the pharmacist could not positively identify for the DEA agent who'd investigated Atlantis—went to a Target with a male companion and found another Vicodin prescription waiting. She purchased it with Atlantis's credit card and left the store.

·

Within days of the Vicodin purchase, Atlantis's two doctors in San Diego both sent letters dismissing her as their patient. But the evidence against her was confusing. She claimed to me that she'd found fourteen errors in the Department of Justice's report, which also contained two security camera photographs of a woman—clearly not Atlantis—with a white male. Both are standing at the Target counter, and both smile at the camera on their way out, the man rubbing his belly as if to say, "Yummy." The report claims that these people bought drugs under Atlantis's name with her credit card. She told me she didn't know who they were, and followed her denial up with a voicemail:

> *I went to my psychiatrist's to get my antiseizure medication,*
> *as well as my antidepressants and my anti-anxiety meds, and*
> *apparently the DEA and FBI had already got to my psychiatrist.*
> *So she knew the story before I even got a chance to tell her, which*
> *kind of freaks me out. And my attorney emailed me a thirty-*
> *three-page PDF file of the DEA/FBI report on me, filled with*
> *photographs with a female and a male all over the place that's*
> *not me, it's not even remotely me. They're even black and white, it*
> *doesn't even look like me, it's actually insulting because, you know,*
> *you would think in the last three weeks I gained like sixty pounds*
> *and got a really, really, really bad perm? Um, you know, no—it's*
> *not me. And you can show it to a perfect stranger, and—they*
> *even made a remark in their report, that the pharmacist, even,*
> *could not identify me with those photographs.*

I've seen the photographs, and Atlantis was right. The woman wasn't her. But did Atlantis know who she was? She told the agents she didn't.

The DEA report listed all the antidepressants, anti-anxiety pills, and painkillers that Atlantis had purchased over the past nine months: clonazepam (Klonopin), alprazolam (Xanax), zolpidem tartrate (Ambien), and hydrocodone (Vicodin). The agent who arrested her asked one of her doctors if he would have prescribed medication to Atlantis had he known that another doctor was doing the same thing. He said he wouldn't, and observed that "when a patient begins to obtain pain medication from different doctors it becomes an immediate red flag."

Still, there was evidence that Atlantis had been used by at least two people. There was no proof that she had written or called in any of the prescriptions herself, and no evident connection between her and the couple smiling at the security camera.

I asked her if the DEA might be trying to use *her* as an informant. Did she know who'd called the pharmacy and impersonated a doctor? That woman Gretchen, who was supposedly making a movie about Atlantis around the time of the Vicodin purchase: Was it possible that she'd had something to do with it? "I don't snitch on my friends," she told me.

It was the first time that Atlantis had flatly refused to tell me something. Normally, she told me everything—too much. Now she sounded furtive and cagey. But as far as I knew, she was guilty only of drug addiction and bad taste in friends.

·

Atlantis referred to her lawyer as "the Johnnie Cochran of San Diego"—though she was quick to add that he was Jewish and from New York City—and told me that another new friend, "my sugar mama in Oakland," had already paid his retainer. I pressed her to tell me more about this new friend. Sugar Mama, she said, was a businesswoman in her forties whom she'd met on Craigslist a month or so before her arrest. She had gone with Sugar Mama to parties while Sugar Mama was trying to get over an ex-girlfriend.

The Craigslist connection and the term "sugar mama" suggested that Atlantis might have prostituted herself to this woman. I hadn't realized that her life had become so unbearable, and I couldn't chalk up everything about her disturbing behavior to her having been abused in jail. But there was also something theatrical in this downward spiral. Drugs! Prostitution! "Johnnie Cochran"! It all suggested a celebrity fantasy—Atlantis as the star in her own courtroom drama.

On April 30, she sent me an email that ended:

You should know that I always have not only a Plan B, but a Plan C as well.
Mona Lisa keeps me smiling :)

Don't fret, Sister—this is my drama—and I shall prevail.

·

Two days later, Atlantis's lawyer secured a three-week continuance, and she posted this ad on Craigslist:

Need a hot, loyal wife? Ocean Beach—31.

Howdy Cowboy—

*Here's my deal: I am a lesbian with two degrees (one in GIS
and one in Pharmacy) but I am unemployed and in a terrible
financial situation at the moment. I do not want to have
children, but I would love to have an open marriage—as in
you are free to do whatever you like and I would be free to
do the same with women. I am extremely loyal, so I would
hope that we would ultimately build a bond together :-) I am
extremely attractive—5'6", thin, brunette, hazel eyes, Irish,
feminine, etc., etc. and I would say other than loyalty my
best quality is my sense of humor. I love vintage/classic films
and my reading tastes range from Tolstoy to Dostoyevsky—
but I am a die-hard Nabokov fan. (Clearly I love Russian
authors—LOL.) I've thought about this very deeply, and
I think I would make an excellent wife to an appropriate
gentleman. So if you're interested in hearing more, send
me your pic and I will send you mine in return. Oh, no
Republicans—sorry :-)*

She told me about the ad and commented that now she had "all
sorts of crazies" writing to her. She said her lawyer had told her that
if she married a foreign national, she could leave the country, and
the court case, behind her. I advised her to get a new lawyer.

•

The next day, on May 3, Atlantis wrote to me that she'd met a "wonderful British bloke" and they'd fallen "madly in love" overnight,

and that he "really wants to be a U.S. citizen. I love how husbands cannot testify against their wives."

Atlantis may have gotten this slightly wrong: spousal immunity means spouses cannot be forced to testify against each other, though they can if they want to. In any case, what was I supposed to do with the information she was giving me?

I had trouble keeping track of all the shady-sounding characters who rushed to aid my sister in her "terrible financial situation." A middle-aged German living in San Antonio del Mar, a Mexican coastal resort southwest of Tijuana, responded to her ad with pictures of himself and a long letter saying that he enjoyed sailing, tango, horses, jazz, theater, and his motorbike, and believed in "life as an art form." In response, Atlantis sent pictures of herself in lingerie, and let him know that she was a "Bonnie-and-Clyde type of lesbian," interested in marrying someone in need of a green card; if they were compatible and he could take care of her, she'd love to give him citizenship. The German Gentleman said he didn't need a green card, and invited her to his mansion.

·

Atlantis found this Craigslist ad:

> *Looking for a wing woman partner in Crime of life. Looking for a sassy girl to be my partner in crime in life.*

She replied:

> *LOVE IT!! I'll be your Bonnie if you'll be my Clyde ;-P*

The Millionaire from Mexico said he was thirty-eight and had a good job and a house in San Marcos, a San Diego suburb, and a background in "the culinary arts." He was seeking a wife and house sitter, was HIV positive and extremely wealthy. His wife had died, and he missed holding a woman in his arms. He traveled on business for most of the year and wanted his house to "look occupied." Atlantis told him she was engaged in a legal battle that would keep her in the San Diego area for the next several months; she told me that he understood the situation ("no sex") and just wanted someone to eat dinner with and stay over sometimes. After meeting her once, the Millionaire from Mexico said she could move her things into his garage. He was a "total neat freak," Atlantis said, and "always changing his mind," but she liked him. She slept in his bed. For the time being, our family could write to her in his care. She gave us his first name, his last initial, and the San Marcos address.

.

While she was making these sketchy connections, I was visiting Crete, where I toured Minoan ruins and the ancient palace of Knossos and hiked the Samariá Gorge. On my way back through Santorini—a putative site of the lost city of Atlantis—I collected stones and shells and ignored tchotchkes bearing my sister's name.

.

On May 6, Atlantis crossed the border at San Ysidro, and the German Gentleman picked her up at a McDonald's on the Mexican side. That night, she emailed me from his "gorgeous mansion":

Am deep in Mexico with the older German gentleman and his smoking hot 16 y.o. daughter.

The daughter is fascinated by me.

Does this mean I'd have to be her *stepmom*??!!

But the next day, she was back in California. She sent me an email saying that she might have found a way out of the country for good.

.

I emailed Atlantis saying that I was very worried about her, and asked for the German Gentleman's name and the Millionaire from Mexico's surname, and for more information about both of them. What might they request of her later on, and why not just stay in Mexico? That was what I wanted her to do. I also asked: What about a trustworthy Canadian? I was still seeing Dan. Did she want me to ask him for help?

What was I thinking?

I was terrified of the German Gentleman, who saw life as an art form, and terrified that my sister had emailed me from his mansion. It was like a bad fairy tale. Surely he'd cut her into little bits.

But even if the German Gentleman was a pussycat, the idea of Atlantis's taking up with any man I'd never met was unacceptable. She'd disappear in a foreign country with him, and then we could meet only on her own terms, when she sent me little messages or whatever. I would always have to wonder about her.

I was caught up again in our sisterly psychodrama, playing my good-sister role in which I had all the luck and Atlantis had nothing. I had a trustworthy Canadian; Atlantis had the German Gentleman and the Millionaire. That was just how life went for us; our destinies were already written. It was because she was born first and had been kicked around more than I was by our father. It was because she'd been molested. It was because she was mentally ill.

My sister was not the worldly woman she thought she was. She was a sad, pitiful creature. If she couldn't kill herself, she'd find someone to kill her.

·

I'd been reluctant to put my relationship with Dan on the line, or to ask him for too much; but I felt certain that I would lose Atlantis if I didn't. So I called him and asked if he might be willing to help.

"I thought you wanted me to marry *you*," he said. I *had* wanted to marry Dan, if he'd ever ask. But Dan told me he had no interest in marrying Atlantis, and though I knew this was a sane decision, I also resented him. No man on earth could liberate me from my primary bond by marrying me. I was married to my sister.

·

Atlantis wrote back that she couldn't just run away on her own without marrying because "bounty hunters" would come after her:

Again, I cannot tell you about the gentleman, as email is not safe. But he has no green card and is very progressive (he, himself was detained by the US INS for THREE DAYS with no food or water, essentially in a bus meant for cargo—so he knows what I've been through). His daughters—

Wait—wasn't there only one daughter before?

—are lovely and he has lived all over the world and speaks 4 different languages. He hates the US—I wonder why—LOL.

Nothing would be "requested" of me further on—we each have needs, though I do have a Swiss man and also an American (long story) on the back burner—but I must meet them first.

She added:

Canada is too cold, and too obvious.

What was too obvious was that my sister didn't want my help.

·

That same night, Atlantis sent a group email to my family with the subject "Mother's Day," saying that Mom had "abandoned" her "for the final time."

You will not hear from me again.

*—Atlantis (soon to have another legal name who no one will
know but Betsy)*

Atlantis wrote to me and other family members that her new name
would contain the initials A. B.

Mom dictated this response, sent through our aunt (since Mom
had no email account):

Dear Lan,

*I will always have faith in you no matter what because I know
you will eventually figure out what is right and will do it.
And you will do it because you have what it takes; you are a
strong and resourceful girl. You have suffered from depression
far more than you should have. If you just hold on long
enough you will get the treatment and the love that you need.
Please don't think you have to change your name. Know that
wherever you are, whatever your name, your mother loves you.
Never underestimate my love for you; never overestimate my
knowledge of what's going on with you.*

Love, Mom

Atlantis replied that as soon as the charges were dropped—and
she believed it was only a matter of time—she'd be filing a lawsuit
against her.

Atlantis believed that Mom had cheated us both after our
father's death and accused her of hoarding vast sums of cash. In
fact, our father's will had been short and straightforward, leaving

everything to Mom. Mom had told us that we could expect to inherit some money in trusts when we turned twenty-five, but when Atlantis reached that age, Mom bumped it up to thirty. And by the time Atlantis turned thirty, Mom had no intention of funding her drug addiction. Atlantis had come to believe there was another, earlier will—something that might have been written and notarized before our father had a brain tumor. Of course there was nothing.

.

One Sunday morning, when I was thirteen and waiting to get picked up at a friend's house after a sleepover, I was alarmed that my father came to fetch me. Mom was usually in charge of driving us everywhere when Nancy and I were teenagers; I knew that Dad must have come straight from church. He explained that Mom had been in the hospital. She and Nancy had had an argument the night before, Nancy pushed Mom—or made a threatening move—and Mom slipped backward onto the driveway and broke both wrists. My father hadn't seen it happen and called it an accident.

After Mom came home, she had to fumble around in double casts, bumping them together to turn doorknobs or the pages of a book. Nancy made light of Mom's clumsiness. She mimicked a struggle with a knob on the television, knocked her forearms together in imaginary plaster casts, and tried to get me to laugh. I told her that imitating Mom's helplessness made her look like a psycho; if she had to play a role, why didn't she pretend to be normal?

ATLANTIS'S FACEBOOK UPDATES

May 12

Atlantis is on the run.

May 14

Atlantis is writing a song for Gretchen called "Tennessee"—
Gretchen wrote the lyrics and has been begging Atlantis to
write the song for months. The muse is at the door.

Later on May 14:

Atlantis is emotionally drained from completing "Tennessee"—
it's very raw and sad and real. She now wonders if it sucks.

And she wrote on Gretchen's Facebook wall:

I love how every time we think we should write a book
about our lives, something more dramatic happens, like I
end up in jail or you in the psych ward—LOL. Two muses
colliding!!

What was up with Gretchen in the psych ward?

Atlantis sent an MP3 of "Tennessee" to me, and to four of her
former bandmates, with this message:

*Half her lyrics, half mine—inspired by her—she was begging
me to write it for months—but PLEASE read the "disclaimers"
before you listen to the song.*

Atlantis's "disclaimers" were in a message she'd sent to Gretchen
earlier that day, which she also forwarded:

*I apologize for the excrutiating [sic], painful vocals—like I
said, I need to record it on a hi-fi device—but then again,
"Tennessee" is a very excrutiating, painful song . . .*

I didn't listen to the song. Instead, I wrote back: "I want to spend
some time with you this summer."

Atlantis replied that she'd found a job—ghostwriting the auto-
biography of an aging rock star from the eighties:

*He wants to do some weird live video thing that the only thing
I can possibly relate it to is "The Wall" by Pink Floyd. He's
taking me out to his desert casa for a few days next week before
my court hearing so I can start writing in a clear and silent
environment.*

*I spent the last 28 hours with him—but at least I was making
money.*

What the fuck?

.

I returned to Paros, kept myself busy exploring more of the island, and had a visit from my old college friend Michelle—now a sculptor and yoga instructor. I had a platonic crush on Michelle, who was well-read and as independent-minded as my mother or Atlantis.

Michelle and Atlantis had met six years before, when my sister and I were living together in New York. I'd worried that Atlantis might find her pretentious—which I knew was how Atlantis saw me sometimes—but she loved Michelle's story about working for some conceptual artist who'd paid her six dollars an hour to roll up hundred-dollar bills, tie strings around them, and hang them from trees.

Michelle looked athletic after her years of physical discipline, and her once-unruly hair had been chopped off in an adorable pixie cut. She had, of course, done it herself.

I took her to a taverna and spilled my guts about Atlantis's legal and personal situation. She said that Atlantis had "a fragile and sensitive soul," which could be difficult in this world and "in other ones," but my accounts of the German Gentleman, the Millionaire from Mexico, and the Aging Eighties Rock Star worried her.

Michelle asked if I was considering visiting Atlantis. I had to leave Greece soon anyway—since I didn't have a work visa, I was required to go somewhere out of the country for a few weeks if I wanted to return for the summer—so I bought a ticket and wrote to Atlantis that I was coming to California on June 7. She replied that this wasn't a good time. I told her that was exactly why I was coming.

"OK," she wrote. "But don't judge me about my weight."

·

In group emails to family and her old friends, Atlantis sent updates about her court case and her living situation. She said she was on the verge of homelessness, out of cash, and vomiting blood.

Oh, I was chained and shackled next to a girl on the jail bus who has a house in Mexico—we were practically soul mates. When I asked her what her name was, she said, "It's very strange—you won't forget it—" and she showed me her wristband: EUNICE. How weird is that? So funny how once you decide to map out your life, things just start falling into place.

It *was* weird that she'd been tethered to another Eunice. But whatever she thought she was mapping out could hardly be called a life. All she seemed to want was money; for drugs, I assumed, but possibly to flee the country. She said she'd been stealing food; Aunt Tina advised her to go to soup kitchens. Aunt Tina also sent a couple of hundred dollars behind Mom's back, with an admonition that it be put toward gas and rent, and nothing else.

On May 25, Atlantis wrote to me that she had a friend sending her heroin "in case of the very worst possibility." And she wrote to our uncle, the executor of our father's estate, demanding a copy of the will. "Don't tell anyone this," she wrote to me,

but I gave a guy a handjob the other day for $100 b/c I had to pay the utility bill. It was so disgusting and I couldn't believe I did it, but I am so fucking desperate and so broke. I just wish our mother would give me my share of what our father left us and call it even. Because there's no way I'll be able to see a dime

of that money if I'm looking up at the Mona Lisa—too many
people will be watching and AB won't be the same AB. I'd have
to get it through you, and god knows how I'd do that.

It was partly my own fault. I shouldn't have participated in
Atlantis's fantasy of disappearing, but how could I tell my sister
now that I would never show up at the Louvre, in any July, in
any year? Still, I could barely control my loathing; I knew that
Atlantis was manipulating me, and that I could no longer deal
with this by myself. I forwarded her entire message to my aunt
and told her that Atlantis needed real help, that I was frightened
by what she might do, and that Mom should consider giving her
some money. If Mom refused, I might be able to send some of
what little money I'd saved from the 92Y and hadn't spent in
Greece. I made an appointment through my aunt to talk with
Mom on the phone—at six in the morning for me, eleven at night
for her—but she never called.

·

Atlantis knew that I'd ratted her out to Aunt Tina.

I PRAY TO GOD you have not told her what I told you in utter
confidence re: the handjob. I am so ashamed and so mortified—
and the worst part is that I was DEAD SOBER while I did it.

I would cut off my own hand before I ever let you do something
like that—but again, this is my life, not yours.

I have my limits. I NEVER went any further than the HJ (I can't even believe I'm even talking like this) but it was quick cash and I'd done it so many times before for free as a teenager it just didn't seem like that big of a deal. Anyway, enough of the HJ incident. Pretend you never heard about it.

Atlantis was right. This was her life, not mine.

ATLANTIS'S FACEBOOK UPDATES

May 28

Atlantis is also in utter denial that she is so poor that she's been reduced to selling her guitar.

Atlantis is still aroused from an erotic dream she had about Hillary Clinton.

May 29

Atlantis is having girl-drama with underage girls and she is not interested in either one.

May 29

Atlantis is wondering if last night was just a bad dream—but the evidence suggests it wasn't—so she's going back to sleep.

May 30

Atlantis is recalling with horror being "invited" to another 3-some last night. She thought those days were over!!

June 5

Atlantis is obsessing over the loaded .45 that's under the bed where she sleeps that she just learned how to use yesterday.

.

She'd posted two close-up photographs of what looked like a pistol sticking out of her underwear. Or I assumed it was her—the photographs didn't show her face. The caption read: "AB's on the run, AB's got a gun . . ." And she quoted a line she loved from *Natural Born Killers*: "How sexy am I now, motherfuckers?"

I was back with Dan, in Athens, getting ready to visit San Diego, on the date that those photographs were posted. I never saw them until after she disappeared.

·

ATLANTIS'S FACEBOOK UPDATES

June 6

Atlantis is obsessing over her growing-out mullet. People keep telling her, "I love your hair!!" Then again, so did all the girls in jail . . .

·

On the eve of my departure from Greece, Atlantis wrote that she was excited to see me—although she might "have to go" while I was there: "The Mona Lisa might be closer than you think."

SAN DIEGO, MARCH 2008

I moved to San Diego to get my bearings. That's what I'm doing here now—just getting my bearings.

13.

On June 7, Dan took me to the Athens airport, and I flew to San Diego, with a couple of hours' layover at JFK. On the ground in New York, I realized that I was very afraid of what I would find in San Diego; I considered canceling the rest of the trip and just staying in the city for a while before going back to Greece for the summer. I could catch my breath and see my friends—my family of choice. I was willing to put up with feeling guilty for the rest of my life. In my journal, I drew a guitar and wrote: "If you die, I will learn to play." Then I boarded the plane for California.

In San Diego, I checked into the Vagabond Inn, a hotel with a pool that my sister had liked when she'd stayed there with Leah, her former partner, the previous year. Atlantis wasn't answering her phone. I left a voicemail, sent a text, then picked up Simone Weil's *Gravity and Grace*, which I'd read in Greece and brought as a gift for Atlantis.

Sometime in the night, the phone awakened me. "Ms. Bonner? Atlantis Black is here to see you."

A muffled pause, then the voice. "Hey you! Oh shit, sorry, darlin', did I wake you up?"

In that moment, I didn't care if she was drunk or pilling. It was her. Just a flight of stairs away.

"Hey! It's room 208—"

"Oh shit, sorry, darlin'. My phone died and I didn't realize it had gotten so late—"

"Don't worry about it. Room 208. Do you need me to come down and get you?"

"No no no."

When I opened the door, she caught me in her arms and nearly knocked me over. She stank of beer and a new perfume—someone else's scent? I held her long enough to feel her bird's heartbeat, then pulled away to look at her.

Her face was flushed, her hair unwashed. She was wearing her faded Old Navy jacket and the same Converse low-tops she'd worn hiking at Glacier Point. Her eyes were rimmed with red.

"I'm so glad you're back!" she said. "So what's all this drama with the guy in Greece? Do you think he'll come live with you in the States? Good thing you're finally getting laid! Did he give you orgasms? You know, we might find someone for you here. My friend Montana's a total dyke but one of her guy friends is a hot bartender and he's single I think . . ."

She told me that the Millionaire from Mexico had canceled his business trips after she'd moved her things into his garage and that they'd been living together in San Marcos for the past week. (I wondered what had happened with the German Gentleman.) If we all got along, she said, I could stay in his guest room while I was in town. He'd offered to cook dinner for both of us the following night.

I made a list of practical things she needed—a place to live, food, money, a job—then stepped outside the hotel and called Mom. If she would agree to send money, I would do what I could to help Atlantis into rehab, or at least into a new living situation.

"Jail would be the best thing that could happen to her," Mom said.

"She says they beat her up there."

"Oh, fine," she said. "I'll send you a check, but this is the last one. When I die, the rest is going to the ASPCA."

.

The next day, I found Atlantis a sublet that would start July 1—three weeks from then—and last her through the summer. I filled a cart with healthy food and nonalcoholic beer at the Ocean Beach People's Organic Food Market on Voltaire Street. On our way to the Millionaire from Mexico's, Atlantis said she needed to stop at a sports bar on the same street.

"No way," I said.

"I've got money waiting," she said. "I did a shift for a friend last week."

"I can't support you if you're drinking."

"You don't know everything," she said. "I earned that money and we need it. Come on, it'll take two seconds."

I followed her into the dark bar, where some dudes were sitting around drinking beer and watching the TV. The bartender hugged her and counted out a hundred dollars.

It took two seconds.

.

The Millionaire from Mexico's house in San Marcos was indeed spacious and was bordered with lush gardens watered by sprinklers. There was a black sports car in the driveway. Before we went inside, I memorized the license plate.

We found the Millionaire in the kitchen, cooking spaghetti and mixing a salad with greens he said he'd picked from his garden. He wore glasses with wire rims, was clean-cut and a bit paunchy. Atlantis went up to him and pecked him on the cheek. He shook my hand and looked me briefly in the eye, but mostly he seemed lost in Atlantis. Over dinner, he talked about his mother in Mexico, and his dead wife, and I decided that he was a lonely man, but probably not a psycho killer. When he offered me his guest room, I accepted.

Atlantis excused herself to make a phone call, and the Millionaire asked me where I'd been in Greece. He seemed impressed by all the islands and ruins I'd visited.

"Your sister's very beautiful," he said. "You are too—but my God, you're so different. I can't believe you're from the same family."

As I was bringing my bags upstairs, I overheard Atlantis talking on the phone. "It's kind of hard to sell myself when I'm like, uh, you know, I'm not gonna have sex with them. So I'm kind of looking for people that, you know, might not be of US citizen descent."

She was leaving a voicemail for an old friend of hers named Colleen, a Brooklyn-based writer whom she trusted. Colleen had once told Atlantis that if she didn't write the story of her life, she, Colleen, would do it.

ATLANTIS'S FACEBOOK UPDATES

June 9

*Atlantis is about to embark on a legal frenzy before her
perliminary [sic] hearing on Wednesday. She also has to iron
her suit, if she can remember how to use an iron.*

June 10

*Atlantis is filling out an application to the Peace Corps praying
they'll do the background check before her trial is over.*

June 11

*Atlantis is about to get in the shower and face the music.
She has to be at the Courthouse by 8:15am. WHO IN THEIR
RIGHT MIND WAKES UP THIS EARLY??!!*

.

The morning of the hearing, we got up at dawn for the trek from
San Marcos to the San Diego courthouse. She took the wheel—
driving relaxed her—and played Amy Winehouse and Arcade Fire

on her iPod. A gray blazer she'd picked up at Walmart was on the armrest between us. I gazed out the window at manzanita, and smelled eucalyptus and the Pacific Ocean. I could almost pretend that we were taking one of our road trips, free to go wherever.

·

In the hallway outside the courtroom, Atlantis called out to a beefy, blue-eyed man in a suit. "Fancy meeting you here! This is my sister. She came all the way from Greece."

"Nice to meet you," I said.

"You're her sister? I'm the guy who arrested her."

"Oh," Atlantis said. She looked puzzled.

"Most family members aren't so happy to meet me." He glanced at my breasts. "But it's nice to meet you too."

The Johnnie Cochran of San Diego showed up late, brushing crumbs off his lapels. I was surprised by how young he looked—we might have all gone to college together.

"Do you really think you can win this thing?" I asked him. "I think you should accept the plea bargain and get her into rehab. My sister needs medical help."

"Let's see how this goes," he said.

·

When the Johnnie Cochran of San Diego rejected the plea bargain, the DA raised the charges against Atlantis to twelve felonies. He claimed there were five other prescriptions of questionable origin that Atlantis had picked up at Walgreens over the previous ten months. Atlantis insisted that all the prescriptions were legitimate. The judge—a stern-looking woman—ordered Atlantis to attend three NA meetings a week until the next court date, five weeks from then.

That evening, Atlantis emailed an account of the hearing to her old friend Tim, who'd played music with her in New York:

> Well I asked "Your Honor" if I could approach the bench (against the advice of my attorney) and she said fine. So I suggested I take a drug test then and there (like I said I haven't even HAD any Vicodin or ANY drugs for that matter since March and before that it had been forever) and the bitch said she thought it was an excellent idea for my next hearing—but *I'd* have to pay for it, not the court. This is so fucking ridiculous.

.

We spent much of that night at the Millionaire from Mexico's pecking at our laptops.

"If this is the same Tom . . ." Atlantis said.

"What?"

"Betsy, I knew it. Look: here's why that DEA guy is out to get me."

"That's his job, right?" I said.

"No, I mean look."

She showed me a photograph of someone who looked like the DEA agent I'd met outside the courtroom. Same crew cut, blue eyes, and beefy face. The photograph was attached to his response to a Craigslist ad Atlantis had posted, in which she'd said she needed help with rent and food.

"We went on a date in February, which was, like, months before he arrested me," she said. "I must have been too out of it to remember who he was when he and the other one broke down my door." She sent an email to the Johnnie Cochran of San Diego with the photo attachment.

Subject: Question re: DEA Officer

I know you only saw him for a few minutes and his hair was parted differently, but does this man look like that DEA officer to you?

I accidentally said hello to him before you got there thinking he was someone else and it wasn't until he introduced himself to my sister as "the officer who arrested me" that I realized it probably wasn't who I was thinking of.

Both of their names are "Tom"—and if this is the same "Tom" I was thinking of, we could have a field day (long story re: a Craigslist date in which he "solicited" me at the end).

My sister might have been paranoid, but the man in the Craigslist photo did look a lot like the DEA agent.

.

By the time the Millionaire from Mexico got back from work, Atlantis was talking again about running away and buying a new identity; she emailed friends and family that if "things go south" and she wasn't able to contact anyone for a while, I would have her information. The German Gentleman had claimed to have a "connection" in Buenos Aires and had asked her to think about what name she might want on a fake passport. Her Gmail pseudonyms—which included "Anastasia Blackwell"—usually contained the initials A. B. If she went into hiding, such a name might give her away; but she said she couldn't bring herself to give them up.

When the Millionaire from Mexico came in, he asked me how long I planned to stay, and I told him the truth: I'd bought a plane ticket back to New York and was supposed to leave in two days. But I'd return to San Diego for the next court date, in July.

He turned to Atlantis. "I can't be harboring you," he said.

"I swear to God, I'm 100 percent innocent of these charges," she said. "Anyway, you're not fucking *harboring* me."

"Look, this isn't a stable situation," he said. "You can stay as long as you're both here—actually, Betsy can stay here longer if she wants. I really am sorry, but I don't feel comfortable having you in my house alone."

.

Up in the guest room, I opened my laptop and searched for a sublet that would get her through until July, when she could move into the place I'd found for her. But would there ever be a stable situation for my sister—would she find anyone willing to put up with her? I emailed some female university students with spare rooms to rent, then rolled my dresses into baseball-sized bundles and arranged them in my suitcase.

The next morning, Atlantis sent the Johnnie Cochran of San Diego this email:

Subject: Plea Bargain

Thanks again for yesterday. (Yes, that judge was horrible— LOL). I'm reconsidering plea-bargaining and have a few questions:

I don't understand the difference between "guilty" and "no contest." Would it be possible for all charges to be dropped to a single misdemeanor (March 19) to which I would plead guilty/ no contest??

If I were to be sent to rehab (and guaranteed rehab) in lieu of jail, would there be a chance of early release?? If I had financial support, could I choose my rehab facility??

And finally, post-rehab, how much probation time would I face??

Thanks again for everything and have a great day!! :-)

·

When we left his house, the Millionaire saw us to the door.

"I cannot thank you enough for letting me stay as long as you did," Atlantis said, "and for taking in my sister too. You're an incredibly kind man, and I know that my being here put you at risk. I won't forget you." She kissed him on the lips.

I stalked out to my sister's truck. She slipped behind the wheel and lit a Marlboro Light; I rolled down the window. "Why were you so nice to him?" I said.

"He's dying, Betsy," she said. "He has HIV."

"So it's okay for him to drop you as soon as he finds out that you're in deeper shit than he thought?"

"No; he's right," she said. "It's not safe for him to associate with me."

.

We got keys to her new sublet, which we mercifully had to ourselves that night. I stir-fried broccoli and tofu until it had a golden skin, the way Atlantis liked it. We watched *8 Mile*, one of Atlantis's favorites. Later, she made me a plate of crackers topped with orange cheese and microwaved. "Is it all right?" she said. "I can't really taste anything anymore."

It was revolting. "It's delicious," I said.

.

In the morning, Atlantis said she wanted to look for a bartending job; she'd heard that a place called the Last Day might be hiring. She wore a skimpy T-shirt, torn jeans, and a wide black belt with silver studs. Except when she was taking lingerie pics, she always refused to wear a bra.

"Is that how you're dressing?" I said.

"Nobody cares about clothes out here," she said. "It's not snobby like New Yawk."

"Take this." I unzipped my cardigan and gave it to her. She put it on and slung her purse over her shoulder. It sounded like a rattlesnake.

"Did you rob the whole drugstore?" I said.

She sighed, opened the bag, and dumped its contents on the counter. One by one, she lined up the little bottles of pills. "These are my antiseizure meds. Zoloft and Klonopin for depression and anxiety. Ambien for sleep. All prescribed and legit."

"If you went to rehab now, would they drop the charges?" I said.

"I'd go to rehab in a heartbeat—I already told my lawyer. But not that nasty county place. You know what they do to people there?"

"I've asked Mom for the money so you can go somewhere decent. She's thinking it over. But if they really let you work, are you sure it should be in a bar?"

"I need flexible hours for my NA meetings. Anyway, I know more about beer than any stoner in this town."

At the Last Day, I saw her hand trembling while she filled out the job application. "Does *La Jolla* have one *l* or two?"

"Let me do it," I said. "You write like a serial killer."

·

The night before my scheduled departure for New York, Atlantis told me she'd been in touch with our next-door neighbor, her molester. She'd brought him up out of the blue, but that didn't startle me; we'd been talking about him for twenty years. Now she'd learned that he had a job as a prison guard at the maximum-security facility in Lewisburg, Pennsylvania. "And get this," she said. "He has a three-year-old daughter."

"Christ," I said.

"But you know what's really true, that I've discovered? Time and dates mean nothing at all. When I try to sleep at night, I close my eyes and I'm right back there, choking. I didn't even have pubic hair when he did that to me. Remind me not to commit any crimes in Pennsylvania."

.

In leaving Atlantis behind in San Diego, I wasn't practicing Mom's tough love. I was simply exhausted, longing for my bed, my books, and the comfort of my friends. I needed that teaching job in Westport, and to get my own life in order: find an apartment in New York or Connecticut and prepare for the classes I was scheduled to teach that fall. It was already mid-June, and I would begin working in August.

She drove me to the airport, and I said again that I'd return to San Diego in time for the July court date. She had only enough cash to last her for about a month, but she'd spent some of it on a parting gift. The paper bag she handed me—with a glittering, winking fairy on it—contained two chocolate bars and a pound of coffee.

THREE

14.

Once, when Nancy was twelve, she told me she'd decided to run away by hopping a freight train. Her best friend, Jen, had done it. When she invited me to join her, I refused, and threatened to tell our father.

"Don't be a wuss," she said. She stared me down and ordered me to say nothing to anyone, even if she never came back.

She was gone for several hours. Mom had a doctor's appointment that day but wasn't leaving her room. I was about to wake her when Nancy came in the front door and breezed past me into the kitchen.

"Did you do it?" I called.

"Wouldn't you like to know."

"You couldn't have gone that far, or you wouldn't be back," I said.

"Did Mom even go to her appointment?" she said.

"She hasn't left her room all day. Dad said we could order a pizza."

That night, she came into my room, lay down on the floor, and began to talk. She said that she never intended to go all the way to Harrisburg, or wherever that train was heading. She rode it for a few minutes, and then jumped off to spend the remainder of the afternoon in the woods with Jen. I knew, then, that she could disappear whenever she wanted, whether to scare me or to feel alive or to imagine herself gone.

ATLANTIS'S FACEBOOK UPDATES

June 15

Atlantis has relocated once again because she's sick of being followed. She's sad that Betsy had to leave today.

Atlantis has routed her course to other continents and beyond and is waiting to hear back from several connections. She keeps forgetting her new name.

Atlantis was finally able to masturbate today, being that she was alone for the first time in a month. I think the echos [sic] can still be heard up in L.A.

·

Two days later, she emailed about ten friends and family members:

Hi all—

Sorry for the horrific impersonal mass-email, but I didn't want to disclose any of your information to the other 100+ people on this list.

I will never be able to contact any of you ever again, except through postcards from various countries.

So if you'd like to hear from me now and then over the next 60 years, or until I am assassinated, by all means, email me your mailing addresses.

I love and miss you all :)

XOXO

Assassinated? Had anyone—other than Atlantis herself—wanted to kill her?

ATLANTIS'S FACEBOOK UPDATES

June 19

Atlantis is planning to do something dangerous today. (Nothing illegal). But dangerous.

June 21

Atlantis tried to go through the looking-glass last night but it didn't work. Her muse is telling her something.

·

That same day, she left me a voicemail:

I just got off the phone with Mom. Don't worry; we didn't talk about you. Really no drama; she was, like, half-asleep when I called. But, um, there's something I told her, and I need to tell you this, Betsy, okay? Um, this is extremely complicated, all right? And I have my reasons. Um. Gretchen did not make the call. Okay? I want you to know that. Someone else did. And it was not me, and it was not Gretchen.

It sounded like she was reading from a prepared script. She was over-insisting, and I didn't believe it. And I felt certain that my sister was getting ready to do something irrevocable.

But I needed to have . . . to like pin it on someone out of state, who I would not ever give up. It could not be in the state of California. Okay? So I have my reasons for doing this. And one day I can probably explain it to you, but now is not the time.

Pin *what*, exactly? On *whom*? *What* could not be in the state of California? Was she talking about the call to the pharmacy, or about something that hadn't happened yet?

So I just want to clarify that with you and Mom. In case, God forbid, I have, like, a fucking heart attack or something right now. And, you know, I want people to know the truth, okay?

Gretchen is actually . . . a really good person, and um, she's hooking me up with one of her really high, you know, top-notch attorneys who will have a free consultation with me whenever I call her. Um, she's really good friends with Gretchen, and Gretchen recently joined the ACLU because of what happened to me in jail.

Again, who was this Gretchen, and just what was her connection to Atlantis? And why would she have more than one top-notch attorney?

They're gonna, like, try to find someone who can take this case head-on with, you know, more, uh . . . gumption, shall we say. Okay, that's it. Bye-bye.

.

I heard from my new employer, the founder of the Pierrepont School. She offered me free rent in a sun-filled two-bedroom apartment on the top floor of the school in Westport. The current tenants would be moving out in July.

I called Atlantis, and to my surprise, she answered her phone. She sounded calm. Maybe she was trying to keep me calm. I told her my good news about the apartment and invited her to come live with me.

She said no thanks. She liked her new sublet and she'd applied for a job at Whole Foods. I assumed she'd changed her mind about disappearing.

15.

On June 25, 2008, someone from the US consulate in Tijuana called my mother with the news that a body had been found with my sister's IDs. The suspected cause of death was accidental drug overdose—there were needle marks on the arm—with no indication of suicide or murder. Mom called my uncle, and for some reason they decided to wait a day to tell the rest of our family. Nobody called me. My uncle sent a group email the following morning.

I couldn't move to Westport for another week, and I was living in a sublet on the Upper East Side of Manhattan. It was eleven in the morning when I read my uncle's email. By then the body had been lying in a Tijuana morgue for a day and a half.

I called my mother. No answer.

.

My cousin Elizabeth called me from San Francisco, and she suggested that I contact the Tijuana consulate and get them to email me the autopsy photographs. I was scared to do it, but I was next of kin, and my mother didn't have an email account. It sounded simpler than all of us getting on planes.

I called the consulate and spoke with a man named Craig Pike. I asked if I could view the autopsy photographs. He had a few questions for me.

"Does your sister have any tattoos or other markings that might help us to make a positive identification?"

"No." As a Buddhist, my sister believed that tattoos trapped the soul in its current incarnation. "None that I'm aware of," I corrected myself.

"When were you last with your sister?"

"She drove me to the airport in San Diego on June 14."

"Have you spoken with her since?"

"We normally speak every couple of days," I said. "She hasn't answered my last two messages."

"Did your sister use drugs?"

"I don't know," I said. "She's mentally ill, and she's been very unstable since she got out of jail. Would you please send me the photographs?"

Pike's voice turned gentle. "People look different after an autopsy. There may be blood and discoloration around the face."

When I saw the photos, I would revise my long-standing opinion that the only person my sister had ever really harmed was herself.

A half dozen photographs were attached to the email. I looked at the first one and saw a dead young woman. I looked at the second and there was Nancy sleeping. I closed the email without examining the rest.

I called Elizabeth and asked if she was willing to view the autopsy photographs, and to keep them for me. I didn't really doubt that it was Atlantis I'd seen in the photographs, but I felt that somebody else in my family should verify them too. And I didn't want to risk having them pop up on my laptop. I attached them to an email saying: "Thank you for keeping these safe." Then I deleted them.

.

I was surprised to learn that my sister had registered at the Hotel St. Francis with a man. Someone calling himself Pascual Perez had given the desk clerk a Tijuana address. Our family believed that the police made no attempt to question him because Atlantis was supposedly seen alive after he left the hotel. As I later found out, the clerk gave them a physical description of Perez—"white skin, long face, thin, with large teeth"—and noted that he wore a white shirt and black pants, "like a waiter." Before leaving the hotel, Perez had told the clerk that my sister had locked him out of room 203—in fact, he claimed, he'd never set foot inside. He'd gone upstairs with her, stayed outside the door, then come back downstairs and asked the clerk to unlock the room for him. The clerk refused; Perez left. The body was found the next day.

Perez must have checked into the hotel with her for some clandestine purpose. A drug deal? A fake passport? I remembered Atlantis's trembling hands and doubted that she was capable of shooting herself up (though she did talk about mainlining in that Facebook post). Maybe Perez had done it, despite his claim that he'd stayed outside the door. He surely knew something I didn't

about my sister's life. When I Googled his name, I found a baseball
player and some dead featherweight boxing champion.

.

The day she disappeared, Atlantis sent me a link to an article on
CNN.com. It was titled: "Inheritance Battles and How to Avoid
Them." It contained a private message:

> *Those Bonner girls just take things to the ends of the Earth!!*
> *There's just no stopping them!!*

What could it have meant? I assumed that she'd left the country
and wanted me to know she was okay, and then died the next day.

.

I opened her Facebook page, half expecting a suicide note—it hadn't
been updated in two days—and I discovered that she'd apparently
been documenting her downward spiral on social media the whole
time we were together. The first images I saw were the gun photographs. One of her posts appeared to have been sent while we were
waiting outside the courtroom, which seemed impossible; Atlantis's
phone wasn't capable of such feats and I surely would have noticed if she'd had her computer on her and been posting something.
Maybe the time stamp was wrong?

Or was it possible that her account had been hacked? I thought
I recognized her voice in some of the status updates she'd posted.
But some of the updates suggested that she had more interest in

taunting the DEA and the prosecutor than she had in keeping friends and family members informed. Her last update was particularly unbelievable:

June 23

> *Atlantis spent last night in Del Mar on children's rides, which beat the hell out of her back, neck, and ribcage. She woke up in the motel room of a vacationing family.*

Del Mar? There's a San Antonio del Mar, the Mexican resort where the German Gentleman lived; there's also a Del Mar, California, a beach town north of San Diego. And why would she have gone to an amusement park? When we were growing up, even the gentlest Ferris wheel would upset her delicate stomach. The rides, the motel room, the "vacationing family"—were these codes for something I didn't really want to know about? I had to remind myself that the potency of her paranoia—and now mine—didn't make anything true.

SAN DIEGO, MARCH 2008

I need to get myself out of this fucking place.

16.

When an American disappears in Mexico, especially if she has changed her name and fled the United States while embroiled in a court case, no one in a position of authority there is likely to care much about what happened to her. And my positive ID of the autopsy photographs was not enough to have a death certificate issued. Atlantis was still expected to appear in court in San Diego on July 23.

My family requested copies of the police and autopsy reports, but the consulate said that without a death certificate they couldn't be released. And a death certificate could not be issued until the body was identified in person, by two next of kin, in the Tijuana morgue.

.

I had always known Atlantis's email password—she'd given it to me after opening her first Hotmail account. "I want you to have this in case anything ever happens to me," she'd said. "But if you use it before I die, I'll fucking kill you." Over the years, she moved on to Yahoo! and Gmail but kept the same password.

Hoping to find out more, my cousin Elizabeth and I agreed to read whatever messages she'd saved, and any new ones that might come in. She suggested that we keep Atlantis's Gmail account active but change the password to protect it. But of course the email account had been compromised long ago: Atlantis's former San Diego roommate had used it to tell my aunt Tina that Atlantis was in jail. And how many other people knew Atlantis's password?

Her inbox was overflowing with responses to her ad for "a hot, loyal wife." One of them said, simply: "WHORE!"

.

And then I found something strange: an account of my sister's death had been written *before* she disappeared in Mexico. On June 19, someone with the user name Don Juan, at robinhoodscape@gmail.com, had sent a fake obituary to Atlantis's own account, with the subject: "Has the War on Drugs Gone Too Far?"

On June 20th, 2008, independent musician from NYC,
Atlantis Black, 31, committed suicide via a heroin overdose in
a room she was subletting in La Jolla, CA.

Atlantis had never done heroin before.

In January 2008, she was in a car accident which left her with
whiplash and back injuries, and for that she sought medical

*attention. Every doctor's visit was documented, and she was
prescribed Vicodin and Flexeril (to which both she claimed
made her nauseous, but at least she could sleep at night). She
also invested in a new therapeutic mattress and did regular
physical therapy to help her recover from her injuries.*

*She took her medications as prescribed until March 19, 2008
and then she claimed she was tired from the nausea so she
stopped taking them.*

*In the middle of April, the FBI and DEA kicked in her door
without a warrant and took her away in her pajamas to the
local FBI/DEA chapter and booked her for "prescription fraud"
because apparently there was some confusion over a prescription
her doctor called in back in March.*

*Atlantis was held in jail for 7 days with no access to any loved
ones since all her numbers were in her cell phone, which they
immediately stripped of her, as well as refusing to let her bail
herself out because her credit card was in her wallet, which they
also stripped of her.*

*The SD County Jail deprived her food and water for 7 days b/c
she was vegan (and would go into anaphalaphtic [sic] shock
if she was to eat meat after 17 years of not ingesting it—same
idea as "mad cow disease") so she drank water from the jail
bathroom faucets and other prisoners would occasionally give
her bread or cookies. She was also deprived her anti-seizure
medication and despite her visits to the doctor and written*

*requests day after day (along with the dietary requests) was
still denied her medication. Sure enough, during Arraignment,
she had a Grand Mal seizure in the Courtroom and her
Arraignment had to be scheduled for the following day. They
took her to the hospital in shackles—and of all things, sent the
ambulance bill and hospital bill to her. They then brutalized her
for "not taking her medicine as prescribed" (what medicine?!).*

*So after 7 days a kind-hearted bailsman trusted Atlantis' word,
being that she had a clean record up until then and she signed
over her belongings (wallet, credit card, and all) to him with
an agreement that he would post her $10,000 bail and she
would meet him downtown upon release and sign the credit
card statement.*

*After that debacle, Atlantis hired a private attorney. When
they went to the first hearing she pled "100% Not Guilty" and
the DA offered her a plea bargain: the 4 Felony counts knocked
down to a couple misdemeanors and 18 months in jail. Atlantis
and her attorney said no way, that she had committed no crime,
and would not accept such a plea bargain.*

*When they went to the preliminary hearing, the DA tried to
plea bargain with her again, this time angry with her for not
accepting their initial plea and said misdemeanor was off the
table and they somehow upped it to *12* felony counts and
several years of jail time. Atlantis and her attorney refused
again.*

Well, somehow this took a serious toll on the depressive musician whose life was destroyed by this "brand new DEA Task Force on Prescription Drugs" (as quoted by Special Agent Lennox) and Atlantis Black, for the first time in her life, shot 7 bags of heroin into her virgin arms to escape being a victim of another meaningless quota. She knew it was futile, she knew it would only back their case even more, but before she left this world, she left a note:

"Dear DEA:
I have had my moments with alcohol, but I have NEVER been a prescription drug abuser. Here is your evidence."

And with that she left a hair sample from before she injected the heroin.

Where to begin? For one thing, the body would be found in Tijuana, not La Jolla. The piece exaggerated the number of years she'd been a vegan, added an extra day of incarceration, and lied about Atlantis's never having done heroin before. But much of it was true. So who was Don Juan? I thought it sounded like Atlantis herself. Or had she cowritten her obituary with someone? In any case, why?

.

The last email she'd sent to anyone suggested what role Pascual Perez might have played in her death. On June 19, she wrote to her friend Psychobunny:

I have 7 bags of the finest Peruvian coming my way tonight. I'm going to shoot it and I don't care if I die. You have no idea what my life has been like since I was arrested and sent to jail. Since I refused to plea bargain, they upped it to TWELVE felony counts with YEARS in jail or rehab (who goes to rehab for *years* ??!!).

And on June 23, the day before she disappeared, she told Psychobunny:

I have a connection for China White—CAN YOU BELIEVE IT??!! The only problem is that I'll have to cross the border to get it—and I am NOT risking smuggling it back.

So I'll simply have to rent a motel room down there and do it there. He has EVERYTHING—literally every drug you can imagine—oxy, MS-C (lol), China White, Vanna White, Black Tar, coke—EVERYTHING. You name it, he has it.

So I think I'm going to go down there tomorrow.

Wish me luck!!!!!!

.

I read her Facebook messages, which included one to someone called Mimi Plaza, who apparently knew Gretchen. Mimi's job description (on Facebook) was "backroom drugdeals and then some." On the same day that she posted the gun photographs, Atlantis had written to Mimi:

*So I have a weird question for you—important to use code
words here: I've mailed Gretchen jewelry that she's wanted
but couldn't obtain in times of crisis and vice versa. I was
wondering if you could obtain any jewelry that I would like
and I would pay top-notch for.*

Mom finally called me back. She sounded exhausted, and I didn't
ask where she'd been; I was just glad to hear her voice. I told her
that I'd been reading Atlantis's emails, that she'd definitely planned
her death, and that the man who'd checked into the hotel with her
was probably a drug dealer. Mom said that we should be relieved
that it was over and that her own grief was coming in "waves." I
asked her how she thought we should inform Atlantis's friends and
her lawyer; she said I should do it. As always, I was anxious about
her state of mind, and I hoped to protect her—I worried about losing her too. I told her that Elizabeth and I could handle everything,
and that she should just try to take care of herself.

I phoned the Johnnie Cochran of San Diego, told him that his
client was dead and that my family would be grateful if he could
return any portion of the retainer.

"Sorry," he said. "That's not possible."

Two weeks ago, I reminded him, he'd seemed to think that anything was possible.

·

I found still more strange information by reading Atlantis's
emails. On the same afternoon as the exchange with Psychobunny,
Gretchen had taken control of Atlantis's cell phone account and

payments. She emailed Atlantis that she'd successfully changed
Atlantis's Verizon password, and that the bills would go to her from
now on. Atlantis wrote back:

THANK YOU GRETCHEN!!!!!!

*You can actually call Verizon and tell them you want to upgrade
my account or whatever—now that you have my username and
password, it should be okay.*

*I know that site is confusing as fuck—it's driven me into the
Bell Jar countless times—LOL.*

*Again, I cannot thank you enough, for everything. You have
no idea the toll this whole ordeal has taken on me mentally,
psychologically, and physically.*

K—I MUST take a nap............

All my love and endless gratitude,
—A

Why would this woman pay for Atlantis's phone?

Each new message seemed to bring to light another shady person from my sister's life—like the German Gentleman. On May
8, they had exchanged emails about what a great time they'd had
together in Tijuana. She wrote that her tampon had nearly fallen
out as she was walking across the border to her truck and told him
to relay the story to his sixteen-year-old daughter. Was this another

coded message—perhaps that Atlantis had smuggled drugs from Mexico to the US? But, if so, wasn't it indiscreet? She knew that email wasn't safe; she'd insisted on phone calls or in-person contact with me about things she wanted to keep secret. Or was she baiting whatever authorities she thought were monitoring her?

On June 13, ten days before she disappeared, she sent the German Gentleman this email:

Quick question: how much would your "friend" charge for what we talked about to get me from "Point A" to "Point B" if things get bad and I need to be able to see all those beautiful ports around the world??

He responded immediately: he would find out, needed to run now, would write more soon. As far as I could tell, he didn't.

A week before she disappeared, on June 16, she wrote a mass email whose recipients included family members such as my aunt Tina—but notably not me—as well as another new friend in San Diego, Jan Howell: "The day I got my Passport I felt an amazing rush go through my body: freedom. I have yet to see the world."

Had she actually scored a fake passport? There was no mention of one in the Tijuana police report.

.

Five days before Atlantis disappeared, she self-sent a copy of her "final Will and Testament" to her Gmail account called Yoursteamroller. Then she emailed it to her former psychotherapist in New York. It was a long document:

(In no particular order):

1.) Her raggedy grey medium Old Navy Fleece to be sent to
[Name redacted].

I couldn't imagine sending Atlantis's jacket to her first adult therapist.

2.) Her Fender Electric Strat to be sent to Tim Adams.

Atlantis and Tim reminded me of Patti Smith and Robert
Mapplethorpe: each had been the artist of the other's life. It made
sense that Tim would get my sister's most prized and expensive
possession, her black-and-white Fender Stratocaster. But where
was her first guitar, the black Yamaha acoustic-electric she'd carried
with her everywhere, with the bloodstains inside?

3.) Her vintage Marshall amp to be sent to Andrew Griffith.

Her guitarist from Drugstore Cowgirl.

4.) All her horrible demo CDs to be sent to [Name redacted]
(along with all her Kurt and Courtney CDs).

She wanted *Gretchen* to have her unreleased songs? Why wouldn't
she have left her music to Tim in addition to the Fender? He was
her best friend and he worked in the music industry.

5.) All her size 1/2 clothes to be given to Salvation Army or
Lisa Royer (if she wants to pick through them).

My sister had been devoted to Lisa, her first lesbian friend, since her teenage nights at Sisters in Philadelphia.

6.) Her copies of Madame Bovary *and* Anna Karenina *to be sent to Lia Jay.*

Lia, a married Orthodox Jew who'd been one of my sister's colleagues at her government job in New York, loved stories about double lives and love affairs.

7.) $10,000 of her inheritance to be paid to [Name redacted] in Oakland (she paid the retainer of Atlantis' attorney and she barely knew Atlantis—it was out of the kindness of her generous heart).

Really? What inheritance? And *had* Sugar Mama paid her lawyer's fees simply out of kindness?

8.) $5,000 of her inheritance to be paid to Erik Solomonson who paid Atlantis' rent when she was going through very hard times when she lost her job after her own mother refused to bail her out of jail so she was MIA for 7 days.

This item made it unlikely that I would ever share my sister's last wishes with our mother.

9.) Colleen Kane to be granted full access to Atlantis' Gmail, Myspace, and Facebook accounts so she can one day write The Book—Atlantis will send her the password in a private message.

The Book, I supposed, must be the story of Atlantis's dramatic, heartbreaking life. My sister must have thought I wouldn't be interested in writing it.

10.) Kelly Donohue (former resident at 39 Nantucket Ave, SF, CA—now in PA) to have Atlantis' PA license plates.

Another neighbor crush. But why the license plates? Perhaps they were among the only remaining mementos she had to leave.

11.) Leah Jackson to have Atlantis' Buddhist Nepalese Tapestry.

I dreaded giving Atlantis's old true love the news.

12.) Orianna Riley to have full permission to publish any and all photos she has of Atlantis—even the ones she hated—LOL.

The photographs my sister hated were the daytime ones in which she looked normal.

13.) Remy Weber to have full-rights to any documentary he finds suitable, including mortifying out-takes of Fred Soffa's footage and [Name redacted]'s footage while Atlantis was wasted.

So she *had* been wasted with Gretchen. Remy was Orianna's husband, and a professional documentary filmmaker; Fred had filmed Atlantis at some of her New York concerts.

14.) Kyle Chrise to have any marijuana paraphernalia in the
"map box" that Betsy gave Atlantis as well as her guitar/bass
tuner (not that he needs it).

Kyle Chrise was her bassist in New York, and a total sweetheart.

15.) Joe Rizzo and Francesca Coppa to be sent Atlantis' books.
They meant the world to her.

Her New York drummer and his wife, a literature professor.

16.) Marilyn Baiardi and Danielle Leo will be granted FULL
ACCESS to Atlantis' photos—that's saying a lot considering
how vain she is. I think there's a pic of Marilyn's *and*
Danielle's old cars in there.

Her oldest friends, from Kennett Square, Pennsylvania.

17.) Finally, my soeur, my souer [sic], dig through my boxes
and take whatever you like. Discard the rest or send to whom
you see fit, like Kyle Wills, Terry Adams, Lisa Royer, or [Name
redacted]. There are far too many treasures in those boxes to
be easily disposed of—and as we know, the boxes are in San
Marcos.

What was Gretchen doing there alongside me, my ex-boyfriend,
and Atlantis's other good friends?

Tell [Name redacted] to burn the rest.

She wanted me to be in touch with the Millionaire from Mexico. It was the only way I'd ever get ahold of any of these "treasures."

Again, my final Will and Testament.

Signed,
E. Atlantis Black

I guess *you* inherited the fortune, Sister!! You'll spend it far better than I ever could :-)

Right. The fortune.

                                    •

I hadn't realized how deeply Gretchen had wormed her way into my sister's life. Her name appears in the will three times—more frequently than the names of any of Atlantis's closest friends. And none of them had ever met Gretchen.

When I checked her website, I discovered that most of the films she listed remained unmade, but she'd published their plots: all involved suicide, murder, and obsessed female characters. I found one link to an amateur horror documentary, which Gretchen apparently filmed at a Warhol-style party; a synopsis claimed that it was a home video of a murder. The Amateur Horror Documentary follows a woman from the back—she's wearing a crushed-velvet burgundy dress, and her hair is in a beehive—then cuts to someone opening the door for her at the party. The woman is teetering on platform heels. Her face is pretty, if asymmetrical. From pictures on the website and the internet, I guessed that the woman might be Gretchen herself. She roots through her handbag and takes out a bottle of pills. A tall, elegantly dressed man grabs the woman's cheeks in one hand—as someone would a dog or a child—and holds her face to pose for a photograph with him. Hipsters in seventies-era clothes stand around the party looking bored and lifeless. The woman heads for the bathroom.

I clicked the film off.

·

I read all of Atlantis's emails from March, focusing on the week Gretchen came to San Diego. I found one email with a photograph attached. It had been sent to Atlantis from someone's phone number; it shows Atlantis, her body contorted as if she'd fallen unconscious, with her legs on a sofa and her face on the floor. There's a slice of pizza in her hand.

Someone had seen my sister dead to the world and taken a picture.

I wanted to kill whoever it was.

·

Just after Gretchen's visit to San Diego, Atlantis sent an email to her friend Tim Adams saying that if anything ever "happened" to her, her guitar "belonged" to him. Her email to Tim mentioned Gretchen's supposed documentary, and that Atlantis had "already" come up with an epitaph: "So I suppose it was just one grand party afterall [sic]."

The epitaph sounded familiar: I searched for it in my Gmail and discovered that Atlantis had included it in her first email to me that mentioned Gretchen by name. "Gretchen flew in from NYC the other week to film a documentary on me . . ." She'd also forwarded that entire email to Kyle, my ex-boyfriend, with a different subject ("letters to theo"). The change of subject implied that the duplicate email was no mistake: Atlantis was sharing her epitaph with loved ones, and Gretchen's visit had something to do with it. The epitaph she'd sent to Kyle and me had a slight variation from the one she'd sent to Tim. Ours read: "So it was just one grand party afterall."

·

I don't know what I'd hoped to find in Atlantis's emails—proof, maybe, that she was more sinned against than sinning. True, the person who emerged had been mistreated, and was mentally un-hinged, but she also seemed dangerous.

On the day of her release from jail, Atlantis had forwarded the details of her experience there (photographs of bruises and accounts of being deprived of sleep, medications, and digestible food) to that Gmail account called Yoursteamroller. I typed Atlantis's password into the account and, to my astonishment, it worked. Yoursteamroller had in turn forwarded Atlantis's messages to First Adult Therapist.

First Adult Therapist was another figure in Atlantis's life whose importance took me by surprise, though it shouldn't have. Beginning in 2004, Atlantis had worked with her for eighteen months. At the therapist's suggestion, Atlantis agreed to try an experimental treatment, eye movement desensitization and re-processing, to recover from her traumatic childhood memories.

EMDR requires a patient to visualize and recall a past trauma while the therapist stimulates nerves in the patient's eyes by shining light into them or guiding their movement from side to side, inducing a kind of hypnotic state. I looked up EMDR on Wikipedia and learned that the patient is asked to "develop a positive cognition to be associated with the same image that is desired in place of the negative one." The therapy is supposed to continue "until the client no longer feels as distressed when thinking of the target memory."

They worked together until Atlantis's partner, Leah, got that job offer to do hip-hop programming at MTV in San Francisco. First Adult Therapist thought the move was a great idea, and she set a date for a last session with Atlantis. But the moving day got delayed, and Atlantis asked if the therapist could continue to see her. First Adult Therapist said no; she'd already filled her calendar.

Atlantis filed a lengthy complaint with the American Psychological Association and subsequently received a letter on First Adult Therapist's letterhead stating that if Atlantis continued to email and call her and her husband, she would report her to the police for criminal harassment. In her complaint to the APA, Atlantis had admitted that during an EMDR session, she'd made a sexual pass at First Adult Therapist, a manifestation of "transference," which the doctor took personally. The termination of therapy, Atlantis claimed, had exacerbated her long-standing feelings of "rejection" and "abandonment."

In May 2006, Atlantis wrote an email to the couples therapist she was seeing with Leah. I have all this correspondence, but I'm legally not allowed to quote it verbatim. It said that Leah couldn't understand Atlantis's obsession with First Adult Therapist, and that the obsession was ruining their relationship and Atlantis's life. To the couples therapist, Atlantis forwarded examples of her own obsessive emails to First Adult Therapist. She closed with a borrowed line of Nabokov's: "A paradise whose skies were the color of hellfire, but a paradise still."

Atlantis was in desperate need of a new therapist, and she would never stop being obsessed with her previous one. And perhaps she wanted the couples therapist to be aware that she could be the next obsessive target if she abandoned her.

Atlantis continued to harass First Adult Therapist for the rest of her life. Along with the "final Will and Testament," she sent an email to First Adult Therapist with the subject "Atlantis' Final Thoughts." It's a meditation on suicide—at least that's how I read it—which speculates about how her loved ones will take the news.

If First Adult Therapist read these emails from Yoursteamroller (which always included the name "Atlantis Black" as the original sender), then she knew her former client must be in grave danger. I didn't envy her position. She might have been compiling evidence of Atlantis's harassment. According to Verizon, Atlantis's very last phone calls were to First Adult Therapist's office and home numbers.

·

In Atlantis's Craigslist correspondence and Facebook posts, I discovered that after she got out of jail and recorded "Tennessee"—that song that she and Gretchen were supposedly writing together—she'd sold her Yamaha acoustic guitar for $150. The young woman who bought it had asked about the instrument's history, and what kind of band Atlantis was in. Atlantis replied:

*Oh honey, I'm no longer playing out—at least for now—I'm—
get this—in the middle of a ***CRIMINAL TRIAL IN THE
SUPERIOR COURT OF CA***. I'd normally punctuate that
with an "LOL" but it's too real at the moment. Thank god I'm
100% innocent and have an excellent NYC lawyer.*

I could imagine how a simple Craigslist transaction might have
gotten personal for Atlantis. But again with the "100% innocent"
business, the "excellent lawyer" business. On Facebook, Atlantis
had made a big deal about completing her and Gretchen's song—
cue exit music—and having been "reduced" to selling her guitar. I
thought that the Yamaha acoustic-electric, its new owner—or even
the song itself—might offer some information. But I wasn't about
to listen to any more "excrutiating, painful vocals" to try to find out.

Everyone is replaceable except, in my mind, the drummer. Because he keeps me in check. I'm the rhythm guitar player. Without him, it just falls apart.

17.

At first, Mom said she had "no interest" in identifying the body or in obtaining the police and autopsy reports, so I planned to go to Tijuana with my aunt Tina. I wanted to secure my sister's ashes, which I hoped to scatter quickly; I was superstitious about her restless ghost.

I was furious that my mother would take no part in helping clean up my sister's mess, but at the last minute she changed her mind and said that she would make the trip to Tijuana—"alone." Was she having another manic episode? No, Mom said, she wasn't. But she wanted to find her truck—the one Atlantis had been driving for the past eight years. The police hadn't located it, and it was still registered in Mom's name.

I reminded Mom that two people needed to do the identification and insisted on meeting her with my aunt at a Hampton Inn in San Diego. I wrote to my cousin Elizabeth that I feared for Mom's mental health; Elizabeth said she was willing and able to fly down from San Francisco. Elizabeth was five months pregnant, and she'd need to stay behind in San Diego rather than cross into Mexico, but she would support us in any way she could.

·

Before leaving for Tijuana, I saw my own therapist. "I don't think Mom can handle it," I said. "She's on different meds—I don't even know what. She's been acting weirder than ever. I think I should do the identification for her."

"You don't need to go through that again," he said. He was right. Since seeing my sister's dead/alive face on my computer screen, I had had nightmares every time I fell asleep. Still, I needed to know that the identification would be done right.

·

Hector Gonzales, the director of Funeraria del Carmen, had offered to pick up my mother, my aunt, and me at the border and to escort us to the Tijuana morgue. I didn't know if it was the usual protocol for a funeral director to provide his own taxi service, but we accepted his offer. It was hot, and all of the Buick's windows were open. With my thighs sticking to the back seat, I gazed out the window at the produce and soda stands, the tequila bars, and the shopkeepers standing around in the sun, smoking cigars and staring at the strangers passing through. They knew Hector—some of the men nodded at him—and they probably knew why we were here.

At the morgue, an attendant escorted us all to a windowless room with potted plants in the corner, then took my mother and aunt into the back. I was worried that my mother might have a breakdown, say the wrong thing or change her mind again, and I'd have to step in. Then I heard a low, human cry. Mom came back into the room bent over at the waist, hanging on to my aunt's arm. "Bunny, oh my little Bunny." She was weeping. "Why does she look like that?"

When we were small children, Mom used to call my sister "Bunny." I was the "Bug."

"It's her, isn't it?" I said.

"It's Nancy," my aunt said. She put her arms around Mom. "She looks like that because she was sick for a long time. She's not hurting anymore."

·

It's the first snowfall of the season—Nancy is eleven, I am nine—and she chases me through the house, round and round the butcher block, until the game turns and I chase her. She leaps onto the sofa where our mother lies reading *Silent Spring*. Draped in an afghan, her legs straight out, Mom looks like a mummy from ancient Egypt. "Cool it, girls," she says. Nancy screams with pleasure and flies down the laundry room stairs and into the garage. She grabs the new blue plastic racing sled and vanishes outside.

I haul out the old wooden sled with metal runners from where it's been collecting dust and follow Nancy out of the dark into blinding sunlight, pulling the sled by its frayed rope. Nancy is always first. At the top of the hill, she stands like a matador, lifts the sled, breaks into a gallop, then throws the sled down and her body down on it. She blazes a track to the post-and-rail fence and crashes into a snowbank.

"That was awesome!" she yells.

I sit on my sled and try to push off, but I get stuck every few inches.

"Don't touch my trail!"

"Why not?" I call.

"Because you'll ruin it, dummy." She climbs back up the hill. "Here, I'll push you." She presses her hands into my back. The metal runners sink deeper. "God, you're fat."

I begin to cry. I'm only fat compared to her, but I've split the zipper on the hand-me-down jacket from my cousin Elizabeth.

"Why are you so mean?"

"Because you're so ugly. Here, let me try." She kneels on the wooden slats; the old sled staggers forward, stops. "This one sucks balls! All right, blubber, you can borrow mine. But don't touch my trail."

I pick up the racing sled, belly flop onto the blue plastic, hurtle down the hill, and destroy her track.

She's on me in a lion's breath, jamming handfuls of snow into my face, punching. I pick up the sled and hit her with it. I'm surprised to see blood springing from her forehead.

.

Still weeping, Mom signed a set of papers identifying the body of her firstborn. I thought she was being theatrical, like those Greek women tearing their hair and rushing at the sea; but all grief seems theatrical to those who witness it.

.

At the US consulate, Craig Pike returned Atlantis's black fake-leather purse, and my mother handed it to me.

"You have made my life a living hell," she said, not to me but to her own hands, clenched in her lap.

"Her cell phone and iPod aren't here," I said. Atlantis had never gone anywhere without headphones. I couldn't imagine that she would choose to leave this world without music.

Pike said that my sister's cell phone and iPod weren't listed in the reports. Nor had anyone located the truck. Mom, it turned out, had made a thorough accounting of Atlantis's postmortem expenses: our flights to San Diego, our hotel bills, our meals. If we found the truck, Mom planned to give it to the funeral home director to offset the cost of cremation.

On our way back to our rental car, walking over the pedestrian bridge to the United States, she took out her notebook and pencil and turned to me: "Your flight from New York: Was that the cheapest you could find?"

.

Elizabeth, meanwhile, was in San Ysidro conducting her own investigation. I got a call from her: she had located the truck in the last public parking lot before customs. The Tijuana police hadn't searched on the American side of the border—why would they have? My mother, aunt, and I agreed to meet Elizabeth outside a Jack in the Box—the landmark seemed especially menacing.

Out of habit, I opened the passenger door, not the driver's. Atlantis and I had moved from Pennsylvania to New York City in that truck. A sheet of yellow paper lay on the driver's seat. It appeared to be a journal entry—or maybe song lyrics:

April

SD County Jail
Santee, CA

I thought all this was done
Cowgirl, run
SD sun
Border run
Border sun

I don't know how I ended up here again
I just have always had this inherent drive
to do "bad" things. To cross the tracks

But now it's catching up with me
The stakes are at an all-time high
To live or to die / to run or to die

Give me liberty or give me death

I want to change my life for good
I no longer want to hurt others or myself
I no longer want to be so afraid
of my past that I keep on running
into deeper and worse situations.

This is no way to live a life.

There were other, torn-up bits of paper that turned out to be a Bank of America cash envelope, covered with what appeared to be my sister's handwriting. I pieced it together.

The message at the top said: "WELCOME HOME!!" with a smiley face whose eyes were double exclamation points. The note was addressed to no one in particular:

> *I know you're incredibly busy, so read this when you get a*
> *chance and then give it back to me so I can destroy it.*

> *While you were gone, the FBI and DEA kicked in my door like*
> *a scene out of COPS and took me away in my pajamas re: a*
> *pharmacy sting when I worked back in San Francisco. I was*
> *denied counsel, food, water and my anti-seizure meds for 7 days*
> *. . . bailed myself out . . .*

> *Since then, my life has become hell . . . I am now living out of*
> *my truck.*

> *I will not accept their plea bargain for something I did not do. I*
> *will see this through till the end—but if things go south I might*
> *have 2 leave the country.*

It was possible that she'd written it to someone who didn't already know the story—though I couldn't imagine who that might be. Or was the "you" like the phantom lovers in her songs?

•

Elizabeth and I drove our rental car to Atlantis's sublet. One of her new roommates had washed and folded her clothes and put them in grocery bags. I spotted the DVD of *8 Mile* among her books. We collected her things and drove north toward San Marcos. On the way, I called the Millionaire from Mexico, and he cried out when I told him about Atlantis. I asked if Elizabeth and I could pick up her boxes from his garage.

"What happened?" he said when we got there.

"She killed herself," I said. "She didn't want to deal with the court case."

In fact, I had no idea what had happened, but I thought he deserved to feel a little guilty.

"I don't understand. I thought she was innocent."

"She was—I mean of what they charged her with. The judge and the DA might have been putting pressure on her to name a drug dealer or something. Listen—I really can't talk to you about this."

"I wish I could have let her stay," he said. "I loved your sister."

"Yeah, I know," I said. "She used you too."

•

Back in our hotel room, Elizabeth and I sorted through Atlantis's things. Inside the box I'd brought her from Italy, we found ticket stubs from David Bowie, Cyndi Lauper, and Radiohead concerts; a letter from our father, dated soon after Atlantis's second suicide attempt and addressed to "Nancy/Atlantis/whoever you are"; a few poems I'd written to her; advice from a fortune cookie ("Think of the danger when things are going smoothly"); and a letter dated May 2000 and signed "Missy." Folded inside the letter was a photograph of a girl with long chestnut hair, dark eyes, and olive skin. She looked about eighteen, and a bit like the Girl Next Door.

Atlantis had told me about Missy. They'd worked together at Walmart and become friends, and Atlantis pursued her romantically. It sounded as if they'd had a fabulous night together under the stars. Missy's letter gently let Atlantis know that she couldn't let it go any further, but that Atlantis was the most amazing woman she'd ever met.

At the top of one box was a fat folder of documents that had once been sensitive: forms from Las Colinas (these included paper-trail evidence of the grand mal seizure); copies of Atlantis's APA complaint against First Adult Therapist; a personal history of physical, sexual, and substance abuse which she'd apparently written for the APA. We also found an audiocassette labeled "Atlantis' Termination" dated 2005, the German Gentleman's phone number, and the contact information for someone named Mark with a note that read "credit services."

And there was a videotape labeled (not in my sister's handwriting):

More than Opium—MASTER
March 15, 2008
San Diego

This was the title of Atlantis's unfinished second album. Inside the sleeve were two sheets of paper, a narrative titled "When Two Muses Collided, or, 'I have no memory of that whatsoever.'"

The narrative describes, in the third person, a five-day party involving Atlantis and Gretchen, and sometimes Atlantis's former
San Diego roommate and his girlfriend. It says that Atlantis made
Gretchen sleep on the wet side of the bed where someone had
spilled beer, and that the roommate's girlfriend had taken the picture of Atlantis passed out on the floor with a slice of pizza in her
hand. It adds: "Where DIDN'T Atlantis pass out?"

Gretchen, the roommate, the roommate's girlfriend—perhaps
they knew who'd smiled up at the security camera on their way
out of the pharmacy, the man rubbing his belly. The narrative brags
about Gretchen's impersonating a doctor to get Vicodin, and other
"felonies without incident."

But what was I doing there, digging like a rat through my sister's junk? There'd been a time when Atlantis had taken herself seriously. She and I had both considered it important that she finish
her second album, for her mental health and for the music itself.
She'd given me copies of the two songs that had been produced,
and six demos, some of which I thought were pretty good. Now
More than Opium was somehow connected to this story about a
stupid drug party with a bunch of assholes.

With the videotape were stacks of greeting cards—at least
thirty—that pictured women artists who'd died. Several of them
showed Marilyn Monroe. All were addressed to Atlantis—and
she'd kept the envelopes, stamped and postmarked. Many had been
sent in care of the Las Colinas Detention Facility, some in care of
the Millionaire from Mexico. All were signed, in loopy handwriting, "Love, Gretchen."

"Are you okay?" Elizabeth said.

"She wasn't even *in* jail for that long," I said.

I put the cards and envelopes in the trash. I wanted nothing to do with this Gretchen or her obsession with my sister.

I put the videotape in my backpack, although I was frightened of what might be on it. It didn't occur to me to turn the tape over to any of the authorities—the district attorney, my sister's lawyer. In Atlantis's last voicemail to me, when she'd insisted that Gretchen didn't "make the call," I thought she was asking me not to name Gretchen in the event that anything "happened" to her. It wasn't as if it could "happen" again.

Would I call the German Gentleman, or the "credit services" guy? No way. This wasn't a murder investigation. The authorities had already made that decision. After all, Atlantis had been seen alive after that guy left the hotel. Case closed.

I didn't want to watch the tape, but I knew I would.

18.

The first weeks back in the east after Atlantis's death were the lone-liest of my life. My sister was gone and my mother had lost her mind. In Greece, without regular internet or phone service, I hadn't kept in touch with many friends from my old life. And one side effect of having a sister like Atlantis was that I resisted bothering anyone but my therapist with my troubles. I knew how boring it was to listen to an unhappy person.

I'd loved Greece enough to consider moving back, and if Dan had wanted to pick up our relationship, I might have. But he'd moved home to Toronto, where he planned to live inexpensively and keep painting, and he didn't check in with me much. When I wrote to him that Atlantis had committed suicide, his condolence note said that he was sorry, that suicide was the worst (he'd lost a friend that way, I remembered), and that I should be sure to ask him if I needed anything. I didn't ask him to get on a plane. Nor did he offer.

·

I moved to Westport and did what I could to prepare for my new teaching job. Reading—once my passion—now required enormous effort. I felt lucky that I'd be teaching young children in addition to high school students, since my first book with my older group would be one of the saddest ever written: *Tess of the D'Urbervilles*. Most nights, I stayed in and read magical books I'd never heard of—*The Wolves of Willoughby Chase* and *The Wizard Children of Finn*—and listened to the sounds of the wings of the ladybugs infesting my new apartment. I liked their company. Sometimes I took walks on the beaches of Long Island Sound. A couple of old friends heard that my sister had died; they visited me in my new home and took me out to dinner and movies. But I found it impossible to explain—or to understand—what had happened to Atlantis. My family called it suicide, but someone might have assisted it. An accidental overdose it was not. My family showed no interest in trying to track down Pascual Perez, Gretchen, or any of the other sketchy people my sister had let into her life near its end. We certainly didn't discuss the possibility that Atlantis wasn't dead at all.

·

Yet after we returned to the States, my mother denied that the dead woman she'd identified in Tijuana was her daughter. Did she know something I didn't? Or was she simply in denial? My aunt overheard her say to someone on the telephone: "Eunice Anne Bonner may be dead. Atlantis Black is a missing person." What on earth did that mean?

My aunt attributed it to wishful thinking—or to a psychotic break. I asked her if *she* was certain that it was Atlantis she'd seen in the morgue. She was, but she admitted that she'd been much more focused on keeping my mother calm than on looking at the body; she also said that the woman's face had been "half-blackened." I was horrified by this morbid tidbit—and perplexed. In the autopsy photos I'd looked at, I told her, my sister's face was pale, not "half-blackened" at all. My aunt attributed the condition of the face to "poor refrigeration facilities" in Tijuana. But I began to wonder if we'd viewed the same body.

In July, ten days after her visit to the morgue, Mom received the death certificate in the mail, along with the ashes sealed in a plastic bag. Mom said she didn't want the ashes—my aunt suggested that I might like to have them—and then called the Johnnie Cochran of San Diego and said that she would not give him the Mexican death certificate until he sent her the police and autopsy reports. He said he didn't have them; but without a death certificate, the case against Atlantis would remain open. When I asked Mom what she hoped to accomplish by withholding information from Atlantis's lawyer, she said she was "clearing her name."

.

I watched *More than Opium—MASTER*, the videotape I'd found among Atlantis's things in the Millionaire from Mexico's garage. It was fifty-nine minutes of a documentary interview, which Gretchen had apparently conducted the same week as the pharmacy crime. It was shot practically in the dark, with a shaky handheld camera, and it began with what might or might not have been an editing mistake: a freeze-frame of Atlantis's face that reminded me of the autopsy photographs.

Through most of the video, Atlantis smokes and sips beer and seems disassociated. She's wearing a sweatshirt that says NEW YORK across the front. Their conversation wanders from Atlantis's music, personal history, and sex life to the ruthlessness of the San Diego police: a cop had given Atlantis a citation for driving with an open container of alcohol, when she claimed she'd only been storing bottles in her truck for recycling. They discussed "Tennessee," that song they were supposedly writing together, and talked about "two muses colliding." Atlantis said it would be her last song, that it was "excruciating" to write, and that Gretchen would be the only one who ever heard it.

·

My cousin Elizabeth said she wanted to focus on putting the legal case to rest. Would I mind if she reached out to Atlantis's lawyer and the DA? I told her to go for it.

The Johnnie Cochran of San Diego said he still needed Atlantis's death certificate, as well as her birth certificate and her name-change form. Elizabeth told him that my mother was suffering from a recurrence of her bipolar disorder, that he shouldn't expect her to send them, and that he should try to deal with the various authorities himself.

Then she called the San Diego DA. As soon as she gave her name, he knew exactly who she was. Atlantis's case, he told her, had been very much on his mind. In fact, through his "liaison services," he already had a copy of the death certificate, as well as the autopsy and police reports. But he wasn't legally allowed to forward them: it was the Johnnie Cochran of San Diego's job to get them independently and present them to the court himself in order to close the case. He'd said so to the Johnnie Cochran of San Diego, who had replied, "Well, her sister needs to get them."

"Sorry?" I said to Elizabeth. "He said that *I* need to get those documents?"

"That's what the DA said he said."

"Why is he bringing *me* into this?"

"That's not all," she said. "The DA also told me the autopsy report has no name on it, and that the Mexicans didn't take fingerprints."

Again, it seemed possible that my mother and aunt had made a mistake in identifying the body.

"Maybe the DA could spend some of our tax money tracking down those assholes who actually bought the drugs," I told Elizabeth. "That motherfucker must have looked at the security photographs. He never should have prosecuted her in the first place."

"But he's seen the autopsy photos and he's okay with going under the assumption that it is her. And he knows that she was ID'd by you and your mom and Aunt Tina."

"Well, I didn't look at the actual body," I said. "I only saw the photographs."

"Oh," she said. "I told him that I thought you *did* see it. Well. I guess that's not important."

"Elizabeth," I said. "Did you think it was Atlantis in the photographs?"

"I didn't see them," she said.

"But I sent them to you."

"Right, you said you were going to, but I never got them," she said. "I thought you'd changed your mind. But if that wasn't her body," she said, "don't you think we would have heard from her?"

I realized that in my panic I must have deleted the photographs without sending them.

"God," I said. "You know how much Atlantis would have loved this shit?"

·

At the July hearing, Atlantis failed to appear in court and the judge fulfilled one of her deepest fantasies by declaring her a fugitive.

·

Shortly after this hearing, I got a call from Colleen, Atlantis's old friend and would-be author of The Book. I didn't know her well, but I'd been friendly with her in Atlantis's New York days, and I trusted that she had loved my sister. She had a strange story to tell.

Gretchen, she said, had called her cell phone, saying that Atlantis had instructed her to do so if anything happened to her, and asking if there were plans for a memorial. Colleen played dumb: she wasn't sure, she said, but the family might be doing something. How had she known Atlantis? Gretchen said she'd started out as a fan and had become Atlantis's best friend.

"But then she said they'd actually only met in person once," Colleen told me. "In San Diego last March. So I said, 'Oh, you're the one Atlantis was protecting. Did you make that call to the pharmacy?' And she admitted it. She sounds like a cokehead."

"Wait. Gretchen admitted this?"

"Yeah. I wish I'd recorded it. I wonder why Atlantis covered for her sorry ass. She said she understood that your family might not want anything to do with her, but she wanted to get hold of Atlantis's music—Atlantis had promised her. I just told her I didn't know anything about it."

"Colleen," I said. "Do not give this woman my number."

.

In late July 2008, I checked Atlantis's email again and found a message to her from the German Gentleman. Partly because I was curious as to whether he might reach out, I'd never told him about Atlantis's death, and he didn't seem to know about it. The email subject was: "Re: Hello, my darling . . ." It was an invitation to a poetry reading he would give in Tijuana.

Hi Atlantis,
perhaps you are in Mexico. I hope you can make it!

Given that her last message to him had been about his getting her a fake passport, this seemed an oddly casual way of getting back in touch. I wrote him from Atlantis's account and told him that my sister had passed away a month ago. I signed the email from my mother and me.

The German Gentleman sent three more messages to Atlantis's address. The first expressed shock and sadness and attached a long poem that he had written to his mother after she'd died. Another was addressed to Atlantis herself, and he'd pasted in a short poem in a flowery font. Its title was "Lugubrious." And in yet another, he offered to share video footage he'd taken of Atlantis at his home in San Antonio del Mar in May.

The German Gentleman lived thirteen miles from the Hotel St. Francis, and it occurred to me that the video might tell me something.

The clip he sent is just forty-two seconds long. It begins with Atlantis walking toward the camera from a sun-filled kitchen. She's wearing a black button-down shirt and old jeans. She leans against the doorframe, puts her hands behind her back, crosses her left shin over her right, turns to the camera, and smiles. Above her head are two gold-framed figurative paintings of a female body in ecstasy— the woman could be dancing or dying. Slowly, the camera zooms in on my sister.

Aviator sunglasses glint in her hair, which is layered and feathering past her shoulders. She wears a silver pendant. Flirtatiously, she says to the camera: "Howdy, cowboy." She laughs. She seems relaxed. "You ha—oh my gosh, you have the most amazing house. I had so much fun, I had a blast!" More laughter.

A male voice from behind the camera says: "Thank you, Bonnie!"

"Thank you, Clyde!" she says, and points both index fingers at the camera. She seems to be having a good time. "Oh man, I seriously may have to, you know, move down here. For good!"

The voice says: "That sounds great!"

"And uh," she says, "you have no idea the pain I'm in right now. But we won't go into specifics."

The voice laughs and says: "Okay, I think—that's a cut!"

She lifts her shirt, exposing her hollow belly above the studded belt. The camera tilts down. She lifts the shirt a little higher in a kind of playful striptease.

I shut down the computer, poured a tall glass of Knob Creek, neat, and went out on the front porch of my new home in Connecticut. The manicured grounds descended to the Boston Post Road. I could take it all the way back to Chadds Ford.

I set down my empty glass and walked to the wine store, where I flirted with the manager. I bought two bottles—one red, one white, as if I were planning a romantic evening with another person—and gave him my number. I went home and started pouring.

Chimney swifts made figure eights in the sunset, and I replayed the German Gentleman's video in my mind. Could the German Gentleman have killed Atlantis, and gotten off on sending me this little piece of film, which felt like a dark movie trailer?

I knew that I had to stop thinking this way—drug lords, kidnappings, murders—but it was impossible not to. What if it wasn't Atlantis in the autopsy photographs? Maybe the face had been Photoshopped. Or maybe somebody paid the funeral home director to show some unfortunate girl's disfigured body to my mother. How hard could it be for a wealthy and mysterious character like the German Gentleman to pay people off?

I told no one about the German Gentleman. Who would I have told? And what would I have said?

.

My head was throbbing when I came to in bed, naked, with bruises on my knees, hips, and arm. My fingers moved to the back of my head, where a painful, cartoonish bump was growing. I couldn't remember finding my way here from the porch.

I decided that, in the German Gentleman's video, Atlantis was not in pain. She was gleeful, taunting. If she'd been kidnapped, she'd done that to herself. And if she was really hurting, there was nothing I could do about it.

·

The very same day that I'd heard from the German Gentleman, Mom told Aunt Tina that she'd received an envelope with the return address of the US consulate in Tijuana. It contained what appeared to be Atlantis's police, autopsy, and toxicology reports, written in Spanish. There was no cover letter. At first, Mom refused to share them with the rest of our family; she said she wanted to wait until she could get them translated. I persuaded her to go to Kinko's, photocopy all the documents, and mail them to me.

·

I checked Atlantis's account again and found an email from Sugar Mama, whom I'd not yet informed of my sister's death. It began: "So what is the story doll? Have you skipped town?"

Sugar Mama said that she was no longer working, that she didn't have enough cash coming in, and that she and Atlantis were going to have to talk about money at some point.

I traced their relationship to March, when Sugar Mama had responded to an ad posted by Atlantis:

> *I would love to help out a woman who for whatever reason can't seem to find a girl who sticks in exchange for basic*

necessities (e.g. FOOD, RENT).
I can't believe I'm posting this, but I am desperate and if I was
reading this myself in better circumstances I very well might
respond, either out of curiosity or altruism.
·····WOMEN ONLY·····

Sugar Mama said it was the word *altruism* that got her. They met up
and hit it off; in their Gchats, both women alluded to oral sex that
had sent Sugar Mama into ecstasies. Atlantis sent her an email saying: "Karma works in such strange ways and I can't wait to see what
it holds in store for you because you have literally saved my life :-)"

Sugar Mama replied: "I do not need good karma—I need a different me in a different world. It is complicated. And please, I am
getting plenty out of this already. That is not complicated."

Sugar Mama's long, heartfelt emails to Atlantis unnerved me:
they revealed a terrible loneliness and isolation, and a wildly mis-
placed faith in Atlantis as an intimate partner. I did an internet
search and discovered that Sugar Mama had a criminal record in
New York City for writing bad checks and had done prison time.
After that, she'd relocated to a place outside Dallas, where she'd
been arrested for threatening someone with a deadly weapon.

·

I sent a notification of Atlantis's death to all her email contacts,
writing that she died at the end of June and that the account would
soon be closed. I heard back from her boss at the California League
of Conservation Voters, who said she hoped it was a joke, and who
sounded truly upset when I let her know it wasn't. I also received

a condolence note from someone who described herself as "an elderly woman" in Atlantis's pharmacy program. She wrote: "I just hope she did fulfill her dreams, even if she did not get to work as a pharmacy technician."

I have what I call goth stock imagery. When I'm playing out and forget a lyric, I just throw in something about the night or the darkness or love or breaking hearts, and it works.

19.

Meanwhile, Gretchen was still trying to get the rights to Atlantis's music. Soon after Atlantis disappeared, she initiated contact with my mother and swore her to secrecy about the communication. As I learned later, they began to talk on the phone regularly.

Gretchen told Mom that she was not just a filmmaker but a forensic psychologist with a law degree from John Jay College of Criminal Justice in Manhattan. She asked Mom for help in conducting an investigation of her own into Atlantis's death. Together they would expose the DEA agent and Atlantis's lawyer as parts of a corrupt legal system designed to make money off drug addicts and their families. Gretchen seemed to have found my mother's weak spots—anger at the establishment and money wasted on Atlantis—and claimed to have an attorney friend who would file a suit against the Las Colinas Detention Facility for the abuse Atlantis had endured there. Mom agreed to cooperate with her.

Eventually Mom told my aunt about it. When Tina let that cat out of the bag, I called my mother and asked if she realized that she was communicating with someone who might have destroyed Atlantis's life. Mom said that Gretchen was simply "being a friend," and asked me for the password to Atlantis's Gmail account.

Remembering that furious last will and testament ("her own mother refused to bail her out of jail"), and those Craigslist ads for sex and drugs, I told Mom that I didn't think it was healthy for her, or anyone, to read Atlantis's emails.

Mom hadn't used email at home, or even kept a computer in her house, since she'd worked as a systems analyst back in the 1980s, so the person who wanted the Gmail password must have been Gretchen. I could not justify handing it over to one of the people I now held the most responsible—after Atlantis herself—for my sister's death.

Mom argued that since she was next of kin, the emails were her property. I said that we had to let it go, that it didn't matter anymore, and that an investigation headed by Gretchen could lead to nothing good. Why did she trust Gretchen, I asked her, and how did she think Gretchen had gotten her number? Mom said she was listed in the phone book, and that it was clear that Gretchen had loved Atlantis. I suggested that Gretchen only wanted access to Atlantis's accounts to delete any evidence of her own participation in a crime. If Mom really wanted to clear Atlantis's name, I said, she could tell Gretchen to save everybody a lot of trouble and turn herself in.

I believed that my mother was in a manic episode—and had been duped. Later, I wondered if she might have communicated with Gretchen in hopes that Gretchen would slip up and reveal something. But if this was my mother's agenda, she never told me.

.

I emailed the one person I thought might be able to provide me with a form of consolation: the young woman who'd bought Atlantis's old Yamaha acoustic-electric. I introduced myself to Guitar Girl, told her about Atlantis's death, and asked if she might find it in her heart to sell the guitar back to me. Her 721-word response began: "OMG!" Although they had known each other for only a few weeks, Guitar Girl was devastated. Her boyfriend had bought her the guitar for their third anniversary, and when she and Atlantis had met for the handoff, they'd become instant friends. She had been planning to ask Atlantis to play at their wedding.

Guitar Girl said she understood Atlantis's depression, because she, too, had suffered from "endless medical problems since birth." Atlantis, she said, was the "tightest" person she'd ever met. But she'd become attached to the guitar; she was sorry, but she didn't feel comfortable selling it. She said that she would name it "Atlantis Black," and told me to drop her a line if I was ever on the West Coast. We could "kick back, listen to music or watch a movie, talk and drink a few beers. like I used to with Atlantis."

.

Had they really watched movies together—Atlantis and this young woman who'd bought her guitar? Between the guitar's sale and Atlantis's move to the Millionaire from Mexico's, there was very little time for a budding friendship, and I was with my sister after that. Why had I imagined that Guitar Girl might not cling to "Atlantis Black"—or be "so sad" about its first owner's death? Or that, when called upon, she'd be humane, have good manners, not write in block text, "The last time we saw each other" followed by "The last time i saw her," as if there'd been a time when Guitar Girl had seen Atlantis, but Atlantis hadn't been able to see her? Guitar Girl, like so many of the people Atlantis had associated with in San Diego, somehow seemed strange and scary. I told myself it didn't matter who any of these people were, and that Gretchen, Guitar Girl, and the sale of "Atlantis Black" were all depressing reminders of what my sister had been "reduced to." Maybe I was wrong to write to Guitar Girl like that out of the blue, delivering the sad and surprising news about her insta-friend while asking for something.

·

The FedEx box arrived in Westport on a sunny day in August. The deliveryman seemed to look at me with kind, knowing eyes—as if he'd guessed the contents.

Aunt Tina had packed the ashes in a red plastic purse. In Tijuana, I'd also asked for a lock of hair—and the purse contained some remains of her scalp. It had turned green. I put the ashes in a patch of sunlight on the windowsill, hid the hair in a drawer, and tossed the garish handbag in the kitchen garbage. When I came back to the living room, a solitary wasp was hovering around the ashes.

On August 13, I received what appeared to be the Tijuana reports in the mail. They arrived in an envelope with Mom's return address. I'd been expecting them—she'd promised to share them with me at some point. I noticed that the name of my school was misspelled ("Pierpont"), which was easy enough to do, though it would have been an unusual mistake for my mother to make.

The thirteen typed, photocopied pages had what looked like official seals and signatures. Mom had written on the pages by hand, adding English translations above some of the Spanish words she either knew or had looked up in a dictionary. She'd underlined people's names and such details as "room 203." It was pathetic to imagine her struggling to understand the reports: I knew she'd never pay anyone to do a translation and it had been weeks since she'd received them.

I put the reports in my suitcase, along with the plastic bag of Atlantis's ashes, and left the next morning for LaGuardia to fly to Albuquerque, New Mexico, where I'd arranged to meet Leah, Atlantis's former partner. At the airport, a security attendant, with gloved fingers, sifted through the grainy material—all that was left of my sister's bodily existence on earth—and I was afraid that I'd lose my temper in public, get put in jail myself.

On the plane, I peeked at the reports, trying not to let my neighbors see what I was reading, but I knew even less Spanish than Mom did. When I got to Albuquerque, I faxed them to Elizabeth and to the Johnnie Cochran of San Diego. If something was wrong with them—if they'd obviously been forged, or if a closer study of them might reveal that the body hadn't been Atlantis's, or if there were any signs of foul play—I hoped that someone in a position of authority would do something about it.

Leah and I drove the winding mountain roads near Albuquerque until we found one whose name—Good Spirits Road—Atlantis would have liked. We played some of her songs to the desert through her old cassette player; I hugged Leah and thanked her for loving Atlantis. We released the contents of the plastic bag, and took pictures of Atlantis's desert grave to share

with her friends. I kept only a few soft tips of her hair, and gave
the green bit of scalp to the wind.

.

Back in New York, Tim and I organized a memorial at Stain Bar
in Williamsburg. With my sister's former bandmates around me,
I stood at the microphone and read Emily Brontë's poem "No
Coward Soul Is Mine." The poem's final stanza is:

> *There is not room for Death*
> *Nor atom that his might could render void*
> *Since thou art Being and Breath*
> *And what thou art may never be destroyed.*

Tim's band, the Teenage Prayers, played some of Atlantis's songs.
On "More than Opium," Tim's melodic voice transformed the lyrics Atlantis had always whispered into the declaration of love it was
meant to be.

> *And I love you*
> *more than opium*
> *And I need you*
> *to help me break apart*

Tara, our childhood neighbor, tapped me on the shoulder. I hadn't
seen her in a decade. She told me she was studying for a law degree and that Atlantis had inspired her to play guitar; she was
now in an all-girl band. Atlantis's old boss at the New York State

Task Force on Demographic Research and Reapportionment
came up and hugged me. "I had no idea that she was so troubled,"
she said.

"She kept a lot of darkness to herself," I said.

Of course she didn't.

·

On August 18, the case of *The People of the State of California v.
Eunice Atlantis Black* was continued, because the Johnnie Cochran
of San Diego had failed again to provide proof of Atlantis's death.
The bench warrant for her arrest stipulated $100,000 in bail. Later
that day, he called Elizabeth and said that the documents I'd faxed
were useless to him; he only needed the death certificate.

·

I wrote to Guitar Girl a second time, asking her to reconsider selling me the instrument, and immediately regretted it. Atlantis had
anointed me her executor, not her keeper. She'd scattered her own
heirlooms. Who was I to decide that something she'd already sold
as she neared the end should go to me?

And I wrote to my friend Ricardo, a poet who was my colleague
at the 92Y, and asked if he might be willing to look at the Tijuana
reports for me, since he was fluent in Spanish. Though Ricardo
had no background in forensics, I believed that if anything seemed
amiss in the reports, he'd spot it. But I didn't think of this as an investigation into Atlantis's death. I simply wanted to hear what had
been documented about my sister's last night on earth in a gentle,

smart, and trustworthy person's voice. And I knew he'd never judge me—or Atlantis—for whatever disturbing information the reports might reveal.

Ricardo wrote back: "for you i'd translate the bible entire into esperanto."

.

Ricardo agreed to meet me after work, by the Alexander Hamilton statue in Central Park; it felt too sad to do this in either of our apartments. I brought a box of Bandit cabernet sauvignon, two plastic cups, a Moleskine notebook, and a pen. I poured little cups of wine and Ricardo read silently for a while, then squeezed my hand and told me, as best he could, what the report said in English.

"The housekeeper opened the door to room 203," he said, "and that's where she found the male sex individual on the floor."

I put down my pen. "Wait, Ricky? There was someone *else* with her, in the room?"

"Yes. It reads that way. '*Masculino*.' Male Sex Individual."

"Another dead person?"

"I think so."

My family had all thought she'd died alone. At the consulate, when Craig Pike had interpreted the reports for us, he'd said that Atlantis was seen alive after Pascual Perez had left.

"Ricky, sorry, but can you tell if it was Perez or a different man on the floor?"

He didn't know.

Did most drug dealers—if that's what Perez was—shoot up with their clients? Had this male sex individual also died from a heroin overdose (which I believed had been the true cause of Atlantis's death, despite the mention of a pancreatic hemorrhage), or from something else? Perhaps he was also on the run, whoever he was, and his death was as mysterious as Atlantis's.

20.

Here is a translation I had made of material from the Tijuana reports of my sister's death. I quote it verbatim:

the place which we attest to see as a building called Saint Francis Hotel, which in the second floor, within the room number 203, in front of the main door, we attest to see a lifeless body of a female individual, in genupectoral position, with the head oriented to the southwest, wearing a brown shirt with the inscription "Good Karma", blue jeans, black underwear, gray socks, and the following physical characteristics: wavy brown hair, small forehead, thin eyebrows, green eyes, small mouth, thin lips, white skin, straight nose—— Proceeding with the body exam we noted total absence of conscience, ocular and medullary reflexes, lack of pupil responses to light and opacity, lack of spontaneous breathing with absence of rhythmic body movements, no pulse upon touch, body temperature inferior to

*the ambient temperature, and rigor mortis. All these signs are
indicative of a real and recent death. Upon examination of the
body looking for trauma, we noted venipuncture marks on the
left antecubital fossa and an incised wound on the phalanx of
the middle finger of the right hand. Within the clothing, we
found in the right frontal pocket of her jeans, two one dollar
bills (US currency). A black nightstand is present to the right
side of the main door. On the nightstand are noted three empty
plastic bottles with labels reading clonazepam, trazodone
and alprazolam. We also noted over the same nightstand, a
glass with liquid, likely water, a hypodermic syringe, a piece
of aluminum can smoked on the outside, with a substance to
be determined on the inside. These objects were picked up by
the expert services staff for their corresponding opinions. In
the place, we found in front of the body, on the floor, a Nine
West black purse, within which there is a multicolor fabric
wallet. Within the wallet are a California State driving
license number B5839311 under the name EUNICE ATLANTIS
BLACK, a credit card number 6018596219606765 under the
name E A BLACK, with the inscription OLD NAVY, a bank
card number 4326302002217775 under the name E ATLANTIS
BLACK, a department store card number 9434030638 under
the name EUNICE BLACK with the inscription TARGET,
a bank card number 4888930232891397 under the name E
atlantis Black, with the inscription Bank of America, two
medical services cards with the numbers 5201890027483411
and 5201890101592072 under the name E Atlantis Black, a
photograph and several presentation cards. Also within the
purse are a passport number 300204943 with the inscription*

*UNITED STATES OF AMERICA, under the name EUNICE
ATLANTIS BLACK, also several papers, literature, a pack of
cigarettes of the brand Marlboro, black plastic glasses, several
US currency coins, two bags, one of black fabric, and the other
one of clear plastic within which are make-up and cleaning
articles, a syringe, two plastic bottles with pills which will be
sent to the expert services laboratory for analysis—*

The Tijuana consulate has no record that this was ever done.

*—a black metallic keychain (not plastic) with three metal
rings and four keys. The identifications found within the purse
have photos whose physical traits are not consistent with the
decedent, given the physical state of the decedent.*

That last sentence had caught the attention of the San Diego district attorney.

*Also found in her body are silver earrings and a necklace
which were removed from the body and placed in her purse.
The administrator of Saint Francis Hotel, Matilde Dueñas
Curiel, manifested that on June 24th, 2008, at approximately
14:00 hrs arrived to the hotel reception two individuals,
a female and a male. They rented the room number 203,
they went up and after a little while, the male individual
(waiter-like) came back to the reception. He was wearing
a white shirt and black pants with the following physical
characteristics: white skin, long face, thin, with large teeth.
He told the administrator that he stayed outside the room and*

that he knocked the door to his companion female individual
but she wouldn't open the door. He asked the administrator
if she could open the door and she said no, for this reason he
opted to leave the hotel. Approximately half an hour later,
the female individual came down to the reception, said some
words in english to the administrator and leave the hotel.
One hour later, the female individual came back to the hotel
reception, said some words in english to the administrator and
went up to the room number 203. For this reason she was not
bothered until today June 25th, 2008, at approximately 12
hrs, when a phone call was made to notify her it was time for
check out but she did not pick up the phone. For this reason the
administrator decided to open the door of room 203 and here
is when she found the male sex individual on the floor.

The reporter might have meant to write *femenina*, not *masculino*—
an odd error to make. But Atlantis would have enjoyed being mis-
taken for a male in a police report.

There are more details about the man who'd been with her:

The informant Matilde Dueñas Curiel of 66 years of age, said
that yesterday at 14:00 hrs, E. Atlantis Black of 25 years of
age, checked in to Saint Francis Hotel. She was accompanied
by a 38 year old man of name Pascual Perez, living in Buenos
Aires Sur neighborhood, who was wearing black pants and a
waiter-like white shirt.

The Tijuana police hadn't noticed the weirdnesses and discrepan-
cies. Atlantis was thirty-one, not twenty-five, and her eyes were

hazel, not green. And had Curiel, who'd found the body, really been on duty for twenty-two hours?

If the report was to be trusted, the last words that Atlantis had spoken to anyone in person—"some words in english"—had not been understood.

21.

That August, I bought a dark gold used Toyota Camry and named it Champagna after a line in one of Atlantis's emails: "I miss you like a champagne disaster." I drove it to Ephrata for my mother's belated birthday lunch with my aunt. We hadn't seen each other since San Diego.

I found Mom in her backyard. She was picking up tiny sticks in her stone circle—a previous owner's garden border. Under her wide-brimmed straw hat, her face was set with the concentration of a physicist working out formulas for the Large Hadron Collider. Mom seldom uprooted weeds; she groomed the earth as she might pet one of her many cats, combing out stray hairs with her fingers. When I was a child, she spent whole summers collecting branches and debris from our lawn, which was almost an acre. She piled it in the game preserve across the road until one day a sign appeared: No Dumping. She wouldn't put anything she found outside, in nature, into plastic trash bags, and she hated people who burned garbage or used leaf blowers. She refused to waste fossil fuels with a power mower and ignored both her neighbors' complaints and a city ordinance that her lawn be kept neat. The children of those conservatives, she said, would thank her in years to come.

Two cats were stalking each other in the tall grass. Mom had named one Joel after her youngest brother, who'd leaped from an outbuilding at his stepfather's farm and broken his neck after receiving what had appeared to be good news: an athletic scholarship to college. He'd left a note saying he was afraid of disappointing the family. Joel the cat got low to the ground, ears back, waving his tail, then pounced at Queen Leah, a three-legged tortoiseshell—my favorite—who hopped away like a giant bunny, clearly enjoying the attention. Mom looked up when she noticed me standing in front of her, pushed her glasses higher on her nose, and stood to give me an awkward hug.

"Let's see this Champagna," she said, grinning her John Updike grin.

I saw that she'd done an incomplete job of dyeing her hair, which fell past her waist. It was pink in some places, with traces of green and orange at the brittle tips.

She loved the car—*great deal! amazing color!*—but we took her red Honda Accord to Isaac's, a local diner chain. She pushed an old Bob Dylan cassette into the deck and blasted "Lily, Rosemary and the Jack of Hearts."

Even if Mom had eaten properly, she would still have been skeletal—she had a thyroid problem, and food simply passed through her—while the few sunflower seeds that my aunt Tina scattered over her Amish salad greens would go straight to her round hips. I had always had more in common with Tina than with the other women in my family. She, too, had been the younger, more stable sister, and she'd looked after Mom for most of her life. She was now a retired welfare caseworker; for thirty years, she'd helped poor people find jobs and collect checks when work was scarce in Lancaster, Pennsylvania.

Toward the end of our lunch, Mom glanced at my virtually un-touched plate and said: "Isaac's isn't good enough for this one."

She spoke as if there were still two of us: my sister alive, our finicky food habits up for comparison. On our way home, we gave each other the silent treatment. I'd long been used to her mood swings. Gently, I told her that I needed to leave, and got in my car. As I put Champagna in reverse, she came to the driver's side window and again demanded Atlantis's password.

"I told you, I don't remember what we changed it to. Ask Elizabeth."

She grabbed my arm through the window. "Give it to me, you shit."

To placate her, I told her the password to the old accounts—though not the new password to Atlantis's Gmail. "Velvet13," I said. "Please be careful."

.

The very next day, Atlantis's Myspace name mysteriously changed to Just Jane. The profile picture was still her mug shot. But the update I'd written—that she'd committed suicide in Tijuana on June 24—had been erased. A new update said she'd "disappeared" in Tijuana, on June 23.

I opened Atlantis's Gmail account. Gretchen had been trying to hack it for days: she'd sent emails to Atlantis's Yahoo! and
Gmail addresses saying she wanted to see if the accounts were still
open, and I found a confirmation email from Facebook saying
that Gretchen had recently entered new contact information on
Atlantis Black's page.

Why had Gretchen changed the story of Atlantis's death? A
tiny, wishful part of me fell into the rabbit hole: I didn't really believe that Atlantis had merely "disappeared," yet I couldn't quite
accept that she was dead.

I called my mother and told her that Gretchen was altering
Atlantis's story online. Mom admitted that she'd given Gretchen
the password Velvet13 in hopes that Gretchen could gather information and promised that she would ask Gretchen to return
the Myspace account to my control. To my surprise, Gretchen
complied.

What kind of game was she playing?

Then I opened the Yahoo! account and saw that every message
in it had been deleted.

·

I watched *More than Opium—MASTER* for the second time. By the
end of it, Gretchen talks over Atlantis and complains about her
failed career as a stand-up comic.

·

On August 23, Gretchen posted on Atlantis's Facebook wall:

I don't know why I am writing, I suppose
morbid curiosity if you were still the living dead.

If I'd still had the autopsy photographs, I could have posted them in response. More than anger, I felt shame—that my sister had let such a person into her life.

But I was morbidly curious too. That night I forced myself to watch the rest of the Amateur Horror Documentary on Gretchen's website.

The woman in the crushed-velvet dress. The tall man pinching her cheeks. The people standing around taking pills, drinking. Then the woman going into the bathroom, where I'd left off.

The woman's beehive turns out to be a hairpiece. She removes it and sits on the edge of the tub, half filled with water, in which a long-haired girl has apparently passed out in her clothes. The woman pulls up a velvet sleeve and slaps her own arm. Another partygoer—a man—shoots her up, and she leans against his chest, blinking, like a stunned calf. The man is chewing gum.

Then an androgynous figure in checkered pants steps into the frame and slides a needle into the already unconscious bather's arm.

A close-up of the bather. She looks dead. Was this really a snuff film, or an imitation of one?

The film ends with a cover version of Sam the Sham and the Pharaohs' "Li'l Red Riding Hood." I'd used Atlantis's cover of the song in a short film that I'd made at Sarah Lawrence in 2000. My film was screened nowhere but the college auditorium, but Atlantis had had a copy of it. This version isn't Atlantis's cover, but the singer sounds as if she's imitating her, singing off-key and pretentiously badly.

Gretchen's website claimed the Amateur Horror Documentary had been screened at independent film festivals in Philadelphia and Chicago in 2005—years before she'd met Atlantis—so it may have been a bizarre coincidence that both her film and mine used the same song. Then again, Gretchen might have made up those festival screenings. Or redone the soundtrack. Whatever the truth was, it messed with my head. It felt like Atlantis was trying to communicate with me through Gretchen; it also felt like Gretchen was making fun of Atlantis and taunting me.

I got up, drew water for a bath, then let it grow cold and drained the tub without sitting in it.

·

Nights were the worst. In my dreams, I'm with Atlantis in her truck, headbanging, shaking our long hair. She turns down the music and looks me in the eye. Then I know she's dead. She's sorry, she says, but she had to pretend to be alive so I wouldn't be frightened by what she's about to tell me. It's very important, okay? I wake up unable to recall the important thing she said.

I told myself, and everyone else, that she'd committed suicide. I just wanted to put the madness behind me and nurture relationships with people who cared about me. To help with the dreams, a psychiatrist prescribed Ambien. But I had become a different person from the hopeful young woman who'd signed a contract at the Pierrepont School six months before; I'd wanted to be an English teacher, but now I feared that I was no longer mentally equipped for it.

I had been working at my new job for only a couple of weeks when my brakes failed on the steep hill of the school parking lot. The brake pedal went all the way to the floor with the resistance of a piano damper. I hit the wall of the school—my workplace and home—and the car was totaled. If the brakes had failed on a highway, I could have killed someone, or myself. I was twenty-nine years old and had owned my first car for just twenty-nine days.

And when I crashed, I was wearing Atlantis's sweatshirt with NEW YORK across the front—the one she'd worn when Gretchen interviewed her. I really believed that Atlantis's unlucky spirit and my own were battling for custody of my body. Like Atlantis, I was broke, tired, and depressed—but I had zero interest in killing myself. The brakes had failed, not me.

The one good thing about that accident was that it prompted me to pick up the phone and call Mom the next morning to tell her about it. I didn't have money to buy a new car, but I told her that the school's theater teacher was selling a beautiful Volvo S40. I asked her for a loan. Mom sent me the full ten grand that the teacher was asking and said it was a gift.

.

On September 26, the DEA prepared an additional report for Atlantis's file. It began: "Possible death of Atlantis Black."

On July 08, 2008 DEA *S/A [(B)(7)(C),(B)(7)(F)] (TJRO)*
informed S/A [(B)(7)(C),(B)(7)(F)] that the American Services
Section of the U.S. Consulate, Tijuana, BCN, Mexico informed
him that the [sic] BLACK was found in a hotel room dead

in Tijuana and the cause of death was listed [as] Pancreatic
Hemorrhaging, however there was a container near the bed
that was believed to have a substance that was heroin, and that
BLACK may have died from a heroin overdose.

Those elaborate codes stood for agents' names. Two weeks later, the Johnnie Cochran of San Diego finally produced the Mexican death certificate in court, and the case against Atlantis was dismissed. When I called Mom to tell her, her lethargic response made it clear that her latest manic episode had run its course. She said she'd asked Gretchen to stop calling her.

.

That autumn I met Nathan, a composer who worked as a production manager at the 92Y. As the child of an alcoholic, he understood my sorrow better than most men I knew. I hadn't made love with anyone, or even felt like it, since Atlantis had disappeared, and Nathan brought me back to life. But while I wanted to let him protect me, I was frightened of becoming dependent, of getting lost in him.

The weekend before Thanksgiving, my mother left me a voicemail saying that she'd applied for admission to a mental hospital in Lebanon, Pennsylvania, but the earliest possible opening wasn't until February.

"I mean, I can't believe that," she said. "It seems so critical to me, and to them, it seems, 'Well, let's see how many people we have ahead of her' or something. Anyway, I'm going to keep trying."

I called her back and invited her to Westport for the holiday. She said she would drive up the Saturday after Thanksgiving. Then she apologized for not "being there" when I was a child.

"What are you talking about?" I said.

"I know I wasn't a good mother."

"Look: Dad and Atlantis were no picnic either. I always tell people that you taught me about words and music. I wouldn't be here teaching if it weren't for you."

"There's a term for what I have," she said. "My new therapist calls it 'dysthymia.' I don't know how to experience happiness or pleasure."

"I've never heard of that word," I said. "Anyway, I love you. See you Saturday."

.

On Thanksgiving morning, my aunt called. She'd found Mom's body, at home, in the twin bed that my sister used to sleep in, and a suicide note on the nightstand.

SAN DIEGO, MARCH 2008

Hang on. Give me a minute.

22.

Once, when I was in college, visiting home, I asked my mother about the time she'd tried to kill herself when she was thirty-eight and I was two.

She seemed grateful that I'd asked. She'd had postpartum depression, she said. She'd imagined her body floating down the Brandywine, felt a rare sense of tranquility, then swallowed a bottle of downers.

Do I actually have a memory of that episode, pulling at her satin nightgown, trying to wake her? I don't think so, though in later years my sister and I would often do that to rouse her from a nap. My father came home from work and found her; then he put all of us in the car and drove to the hospital.

.

In the early 1980s, my grandmother inherited the farm on Gum Tree Road after her second husband, Mom's stepfather, died of heart failure. She sold it immediately, without asking any of her children if they might like to buy it from her. Mom had long dreamed of living close to the earth, and she always resented not having been given a chance to hold on to the farm. Sometimes, when Nancy and I were children, Mom would drive us by the place and tell us that it could have been ours. I knew Mom had recovered from her first nervous breakdown on that farm, when she was in her twenties, and that it was where her brother Joel had jumped off the roof and broken his neck.

I'd found it strange that my mother wanted to live among such memories. Now I believe that it must have been one of the only tranquil places she'd ever known.

.

Stories about suicide in my mother's family go back at least one generation before her and Joel. My great-aunt Rebecca, an unmarried schoolteacher who lived with her mother and her two brothers, was said to have jumped off a bridge in Philadelphia in the 1940s. She may have been mourning her brother John, who'd supposedly shot himself to death a few years before. Perhaps because the family didn't want the shame of yet another suicide, nobody claimed Rebecca's body.

Atlantis and I didn't learn about Rebecca—or about the others in my mother's family—until a year or so before Atlantis disappeared. "Why didn't you tell us?" she said to our mother. "All those years I was depressed, I could have felt less alone."

Give me another minute.

[Atlantis puts her hands in her hair, covers her face.]

23.

My mother died of multiple-drug toxicity. The suicide note appeared to have been written in her own hand, though the writing looked unusually large. I immediately thought: *My sister killed her.* But of course I banished that thought. What had happened to my sister killed her. I told myself the script in her suicide note looked large only in the photocopy that the police had given my aunt. (They kept the original.) And she was probably on drugs when she'd written it.

Still, I couldn't forget Nancy's imitations of my mother's handwriting: those forged notes excusing her from school.

.

The suicide note was addressed "To the ones I love," and said: "We are all relieved of a tragic burden." It contained an apology without specifying for what. Then it addressed me directly and told me please not to worry about her—"I am not worried about you." I would have "a good life," the note said, and was "on my way." It ended with a sentence in the past tense: "If I saw any option at all, I would have taken it."

·

Of course I imagined that the note was a forgery, a message from Atlantis. It meant that *she* was still alive, and that I shouldn't worry about her. The apology was for killing our mother.

And of course it wasn't possible. Atlantis was dead, I told myself. Yet I held her entirely responsible.

·

To my knowledge, Mom hadn't had plans to see anyone that day, but she was wearing makeup when she died. Aunt Tina had invited Mom to join her and Tina's two stepdaughters for a holiday lunch—a sort of orphans' Thanksgiving—and Mom had declined. But Tina showed up that morning anyway, along with her stepdaughters. She told them—and, later on, the police—that she'd felt an urgent need to visit her sister for a "mental health check," and that she was worried because Mom hadn't picked up the phone.

·

The story I told myself was that Atlantis had committed suicide as a protest against the DEA, and that my mother had followed suit. The story I told only to myself, and kept to myself, was that even if Atlantis hadn't really died in Tijuana, she couldn't have managed to live much longer "on the run." Not with Sugar Mama wanting her money back. Not with people like Gretchen and the German Gentleman involving themselves in her life.

·

A few days after Thanksgiving, Gretchen called my cell phone and left two messages saying that she needed to speak to me urgently. The third time she called, I picked up.

"I know you probably don't want to hear from me," she said, "but I wanted to express my condolences about your mother. I was worried that something had happened, and I was calling and calling her house, until finally a neighbor picked up the phone and told me that she'd passed."

Really? It was unlikely that my mother's nonagenarian neighbor, Lenore, would have been in my mother's house at all—much less picked up her phone. I assumed instead that Gretchen must somehow have seen the obituary published in the *Lancaster Intelligencer*. But why would a New Yorker have been reading that paper? Or had Gretchen been Googling my mother's name? I didn't want to think about it.

"Listen: Gretchen? I can't talk to you. Thanks anyway for the condolences."

"I wanted to reach out to you after Atlantis disappeared," she went on in a flat, steamrolling voice, as if I hadn't spoken. "She gave me special instructions—but your mother said you didn't want to hear from me. But I feel your mother's loss very deeply, and of course you know I still feel Atlantis's too."

"I have a lot to take care of here," I said. "Please don't call me again."

．

When I hung up, I thought about consulting a private investigator; after what had happened to my sister, I didn't trust the police. But the last thing I wanted was to get a possible psychopath more interested in me, or to make her think I was afraid of her. I couldn't quite believe that Gretchen had literally killed my sister or my mother, but this wannabe snuff filmmaker, self-declared forensic psychologist, and stalker of my family was obviously a terrible person. I believed that my sister had been used, and my mother harassed, by someone who seemed to have no boundaries at all.

I thought about changing my number, and even my name. But that would only prove that she had gotten under my skin. The best course of action for my own mental health was to forget Gretchen.

．

I tried my luck once more with Guitar Girl. "Last request with more sad news" was my email subject. I informed her that my mother had died of grief, and that even though I'd never be okay, I still wanted my sister's guitar to hold in both of their absences. I needed something. It would mean more to me now, I wrote, than it ever had. I told Guitar Girl to name her price.

I didn't tell Guitar Girl that my mother had played bluegrass banjo, or that we'd smoked pot together at a Bob Dylan and Willie

Nelson concert in Reading and gone to two Patti Smith concerts in Brooklyn.

Nor did I mention that song called "Tennessee" that Atlantis and Gretchen had written together; or that after finally listening to the unlistenable, and understanding its lyrics (sort of), I believed that Atlantis's guitar contained some powerful demons that needed exorcising. Guitar Girl had no idea what a favor I was offering her.

I didn't hear back from her right away.

.

Over Christmas, I met my aunt to finish cleaning out my mother's house. Swallowing my dread, I climbed the steep stairs, creaked open the door to the room my mother died in, and found Queen Leah, the tripod kitty, curled up on the bedspread, facing the door, as if she had been expecting me.

She rubbed her face on my hands, purred, licked me, rolled onto her back, and stretched her phantom limb. It comforted me to know that Queen Leah had been with my mother when she died. I had never wished so hard to understand the language of animals.

.

I went through some boxes of documents and papers that my aunt had found. There were letters that had been typed on a word processor, apparently signed by my mother, and then photocopied. Normally, she used a typewriter since she didn't have a computer. One, dated August 11, 2008, was addressed to Sr. Hector M.

Gonzales Valencia, the director of Funeraria del Carmen, where Atlantis's body had been taken. At the top, she'd handwritten an explanation:

(my letter to introduce Gretchen to Hector)

Dear Hector,

You may be surprised to hear from me again so soon. The fact is, I need a favor from you, my friend in Mexico.

Attorneys in New York and California are investigating two San Diego lawyers involved in a prescription-drug fraud case against my daughter, the late Atlantis Black. The investigators are four young women—three in New York City and one in San Diego. (Two are attorneys; one is a law student; one is a film maker who has a degree in Forensic Psychology and a native Spanish speaker for a business partner.)

After studying the Police and Autopsy Reports regarding my daughter, the investigators have questions that only the Mexican officials can answer.

The investigators need a bilingual contact person in Tijuana— someone sophisticated enough to deal with the bureaucracy, but low-profile enough not to attract attention (one of your sons, perhaps?)

The person who would like to call you is the film maker,
Gretchen, in New York. Thank you in advance for your kind
attention to this delicate matter.

Sincerely yours,
Beth Bonner

What possible business could Gretchen have with my sister's funeral director? And if her field was forensics—and she had a native Spanish speaker as a "business partner"—might she have had
a hand in my sister's autopsy and toxicology reports? Could this
letter itself have been forged?

At the bottom of the box, I found a stack of vintage copies
of the *Ladder*, a lesbian magazine, published by the Daughters of
Bilitis; and a photocopy of a 106-page novella, *Autumn*, a coming-
out tale Atlantis had written when she was twenty. The title character is beautiful, green-eyed, obsessive, and relentless, fleeing the
East Coast and her troubled past. Several other female characters,
including an attractive hitchhiker and an old woman who uses a
wheelchair in a mental hospital, also have green eyes. The two who
don't are Margarita, a Mexican American teenager whom Autumn
meets in a psych ward and has hot sex with under the stars; and
Randy, a mechanic with whom Autumn has a one-night stand in a
chapter called, strangely enough, "Tennessee."

But I'd read Atlantis's manuscript before, and I remembered it
as having had fewer characters and a different ending. It seemed
unlikely that Atlantis would have rewritten her novella—if my rec-
ollection was accurate—and left a copy in our mother's house. It
seemed like something that Gretchen might have done; she was

forever trying to change my sister's story. It was eerie that my sister's writing and Gretchen's handiwork were blending in reality. I no longer knew my sister's own words. *Two muses colliding*.

.

A few weeks before her death, Mom had changed her will. She'd kept me as a beneficiary, and in Atlantis's place, she'd named my aunt Tina. That will was notarized in my aunt's presence. Then she changed it again, decreasing my aunt's portion from 50 percent to 25 percent and leaving the other 25 percent to Leah, Atlantis's former partner. My aunt said that Mom had told her about it, but these changes hadn't been notarized. It was odd that Mom had written Leah into her will at all; still, it seemed like something Atlantis would have wanted. I called Leah to tell her that my mother had died, and that she'd wanted to leave her a portion of the estate that had originally been for Atlantis. Leah wept when I said that Mom had committed suicide. She graciously declined any of my mother's money, which ended up going to me.

*I guess *you* inherited the fortune, Sister!!*

I considered taking a leave of absence from my job and traveling. But I wouldn't have the money for months, and there wasn't anywhere I wanted to go. So, instead, I said yes to as many social invitations as I could and established a strict routine: I worked during the week, took afternoon walks in the park, prepared for classes on weeknights with Queen Leah curled up beside me. She'd purr and lick my hand, as if it were my mother's hand.

.

I heard back from Guitar Girl:

> *she and i didn't have more than a few months to get to know*
> *each other but we became very personal very quick because we*
> *understood each other. i was dealing with a lot personally when*
> *i met her, she was the exact person i needed to meet and speak*
> *to . . .*

Either Guitar Girl had a faulty memory or something was up. She and Atlantis first corresponded after "meeting" on Craigslist on May 26. They certainly hadn't had "a few months." I wondered if Guitar Girl might in fact be Gretchen.

·

Nathan and I had been dating for only six weeks when my mother died. We spent nights together listening to music, eating takeout, and making love. One weekend, we took a road trip to Vermont and stayed on a farm. We went out after midnight to smoke a joint, stood in a meadow with horses and dark mountains all around, and I felt safe for the first time in months.

Guitar Girl finally took pity on me and sold me my sister's acoustic for the price she'd paid. "Atlantis Black" arrived by UPS on the last day of the year. Guitar Girl had put a sticker on its case, which was falling apart. It said: "Aloha."

With "Atlantis Black" in my possession, I invited Nathan over for New Year's Eve—he played beautifully—and we sang every song we could think of. In the morning, I crept out of bed while he slept, put the instrument back in its case, fastened the snaps, and tucked it in a corner of my living room. A minute later, I got up again and hid it behind a thatch of dresses in my closet.

.

In January 2009, Nathan won silver tickets to Barack Obama's inauguration. I took the day off from school and joined him in DC. After the ceremony, Nathan and I got drunk on the train to his uncle's house in Silver Spring, Maryland; that night, by accident, I became pregnant.

A part of me wanted to have that baby. When the doctor showed us the beating heart on the sonogram, Nathan held my hand, and I cried. We talked about becoming parents together. While she was still in my womb, we named her Virginia, after Nathan's grandmother. I imagined raising a dream-child and giving her a dream-education at the dream-school where I worked.

But I wasn't ready. I prayed that Virginia might be spared whatever bad gene had passed from my mother to my sister, but how could I be sure? Even as I wished for that child, I felt unable to take such a risk. I could not give birth to another Atlantis.

I got it—my next album will be called Glamor. *Spelled the American English way, not the British. Glamor is just a Midwestern girl who wants to get to Hollywood. But she doesn't make it.*

24.

In 2010, twenty-three police and public officials in Tijuana were dismissed on charges of corruption, some of them for working with kidnappers and extortionists. Among the dismissed officers was Felipe Ortega Becerra, who'd been in charge of investigating my sister's death.

·

In 2012, Ernesto Haberli of Avidhosting.com was ordered to pay half a million dollars in restitution for seven counts of mail fraud. The prosecution was a result of an investigation into Avidhosting.com by the United States Postal Inspection Service and the FBI.

I had suspected that Atlantis's lawsuit was righteous but quixotic. But had she not been in touch with the FBI just before her own life became too consuming to do free legal work, it's conceivable that Haberli might have escaped punishment. Haberli had allegedly sold domain names to criminals in cyberspace, and there were plenty of hackers who could have had easy access to information about Atlantis—not only her credit card but her taste for opiates. But this speculation—that Atlantis's arrest might have had anything to do with her lawsuit against Haberli—was another dead end. By the time of Haberli's conviction, Atlantis's domain name had long since expired. It was as if her home page, Atlantisblack.com, had never existed.

.

I didn't spend a lot of time searching for Atlantis in the "bit roles and extra parts" she claimed to have played in the Samuel L. Jackson, Matthew McConaughey, and Ashton Kutcher movies made in LA in early 2008. But after she'd been gone a few years, I found that abysmal version of *As You Like It* on Vimeo. The biggest name in it was Victoria Mature. I watched it for ten minutes, and there was Atlantis.

Atlantis plays "Duke Frederick's Date." A silent role, of course. A woman without a name. She wears that heavy eyeliner we'd both used in high school. The bright red lipstick she'd put on for our father's funeral. She's in a fancy dress with a halter top. I'd never seen my sister look so feminine. Her breasts appear to have been taped up to create cleavage.

Duke Frederick and his Date are at a wrestling match. Atlantis feigns interest in the men straddling each other. She's clearly *acting*; maybe her character is supposed to be bored. But the director must have noticed that Atlantis was camera-friendly, because she appears again in the next scene. She's at an event to pay the winner, or someone who'd bet on the fight, and she's holding an oversized check, like Vanna White on *Wheel of Fortune*.

Bad as the film is, I loved seeing her immortalized through a professional's lens rather than in that mug shot of April 2008, in the German Gentleman's forty-two-second clip, or in Gretchen's shaky video. *As You Like It* had been filmed three months before her disappearance. She looks as if she will always be beautiful, shaking her dark hair, holding up that outlandishly huge check.

·

I brought "Atlantis Black" to a guitar whisperer in North Adams, Massachusetts, to get it fixed up. He asked if I wanted to keep the "claw marks"—white streaks embedded in the black finish around the sound hole. I said yes. He lowered the action and replaced the plastic nut with bone—of some animal, I guess. I've lent "Atlantis Black" to my friends to play, and I've tried to learn myself. But it hurts my fingers. Most of the time it rests in a hard black case lined with green velvet.

Once upon a time, I hoped that Atlantis's songs might be "discovered"—produced by some genius or covered by a famous singer. After she gave up on her music, their release was hardly a priority for her, or, later, for me. In fact, by going against my sister's last wishes ("All her horrible demo CDs to be sent to Gretchen") and keeping those demos in the dark, I prevented it from happening. I doubted that anybody famous would have been interested.

Before she gave up, Atlantis had wanted to be admired—or at least heard and looked at—and remembered. This book is, in part, my way of doing that for her. Of course it's not entirely a tribute. There was a rivalry between us, and she caused me a world of pain. I'm the one who survived to tell the story.

Certainly I felt sadness—and shame—over what became of her; but I'm also proud of what she managed to accomplish.

Maybe she truly was gifted and undermined herself so badly that the music turned out to be unsalvageable. It's important to know, because that was her life—until it wasn't. But I really don't know. Back when I was a teenager, she convinced me that she was serious, that she was an artist. But when I got to Sarah Lawrence, my film teacher listened to her cover of "Li'l Red Riding Hood" and said, "Why doesn't she just actually sing? In her real voice? She sounds pretentious." I was mortified. But while I understood what the teacher meant, I also thought: *Don't you see how amazing it is that she can even do this?*

Was she once a promising songwriter? Ultimately, why does that matter? If Atlantis was her best self when she was writing, practicing, performing, and recording music, wasn't that of value? I was afraid of what might happen to her if she stopped playing. And I was right. It was better, for both of us, when the worst she might do was sing as if she were dying.

.

In June 2013—five years after Atlantis's disappearance—I discovered that I had become Facebook friends with "Maggie." She hadn't sent me a friend request—somehow she'd just appeared among my other friends. She had the generic blue-and-white identification image of someone who'd put her account on hold or was just starting out.

I clicked on the profile icon. "Maggie's" page turned out to be Atlantis's old page, exhumed and subtly altered. Whoever "Maggie" was, she had reposted Atlantis's final, alarming updates. "Atlantis has relocated once again because she's sick of being followed." I checked Atlantis's Gmail account. Sure enough, Gretchen's address had hacked it at last, and had used it to resurrect my sister's disabled Facebook page.

I clicked "unfriend."

On the Fourth of July—the date on Atlantis's death certificate—a new fan page on Facebook appeared in her memory, with photographs lifted from both my personal Facebook account and Atlantis's old Myspace page. I jumped back from the screen when I saw family pictures taken at our house in Chadds Ford: Atlantis at age two, in footed pajamas, playing her rainbow-striped toy guitar; Atlantis smiling shyly at age nine, in an oversized red T-shirt, cradling Tyger, our first cat, in her thin arms. My mother and I had snapped those photographs. I had put them up myself, back when people didn't worry about Facebook's owning everything they posted. Seeing my family's photographs used in this way felt like *Zersetzung*—the Stalinist terror practice of secretly rearranging your furniture and private things when you weren't at home to make you fear you'd lost your mind.

Though the host of this new page did not provide her name or contact information anywhere, she claimed she was "Atlantis's best friend, from 2005 until the day before she disappeared— June 23, 2008." That was the day Gretchen had taken control of Atlantis's cell phone account. The host said that the best way to describe their relationship was "folie a deux." And the host mentioned that after Atlantis disappeared, she spoke "everyday [*sic*]" with Atlantis's mother until she died. Atlantis's mother, the host wrote, was "fascinating."

I owed my sister's *and* my mother's ghosts an intervention.

I cyberstalked Gretchen and discovered that she kept a blog that linked to an "Atlantis Black" channel on YouTube. The channel contained a few videos of Atlantis's live shows and a link to a collection of photographs called "The Homeless of New York": images of street people and their pets. These images were for sale on eBay, and the seller's bio said that she was a forensic psychologist. I did some more digging and saw that on Amazon, Gretchen had given high praise to a product called Mr. Clean Magic Eraser Kitchen and Dish Scrubber.

I wrote to Facebook, explained who I was, and asked them to remove Gretchen's fan page. After a few days, someone made it disappear.

.

In May 2015, when I'd finished my first collection of poems—mostly elegies for my family—and had begun writing this book, I reached out for the first time to Gretchen.

When she called me back, she sounded breathless and rushed in to fill my silences. She started in about the rights to Atlantis's music. Before I could respond, she asked me if my mother had really committed suicide. I told her that was what the death certificate said.

"That's what I thought." I could have sworn that she sounded pleased.

She said that she'd talked to my mother on the phone nearly every day toward the end of her life, and that my mother had seemed especially depressed because she hadn't had plans for the holiday.

I said that Mom was depressed, but not about not having Thanksgiving plans.

I asked how she and Atlantis had met; she said she first heard Atlantis on the radio—then corrected herself, saying that she *never* listened to the radio—and that after hearing a particular lyric—she didn't say which one—she had her "producer" get in touch with Atlantis. It was Gretchen's own idea, Gretchen claimed, for Atlantis to do a cover of Bruce Springsteen's "I'm on Fire."

I said I thought she'd first reached out to Atlantis as a documentary filmmaker; she said no, she really only had "that one thing on the web," and she thought of herself as "more of a writer."

Why had she changed Atlantis's Verizon password, I asked her, and taken responsibility for her cell phone bill? Because Atlantis had no money, she said, and she herself was rich. She'd have happily bailed Atlantis out of jail, she said, but she'd been in rehab at the time. But she now had a wonderful therapist, who'd helped her survive her own childhood trauma: she'd been gang-raped at the age of six, then forced into prostitution by her father.

I said I was sorry that had happened to her.

She told me that she knew Atlantis hadn't died in Tijuana the way the reports said. And she had a "big, fat file" of information about the prescription drug case against Atlantis—information she wasn't "even supposed to have." Might she be willing to share it? Sure, she said. I asked if we could meet. Yes, she said, but could she call me back? Her four-year-old niece was at the door—it was the little girl's birthday.

·

A couple of weeks later, in June 2015, I visited my aunt Tina in Lancaster, Pennsylvania. She still had a few boxes of documents and papers from my mother's house stored in her basement. I'd never sorted through them all. I opened one box on my aunt's dining room table; multiple copies of what looked like brochures advertising Atlantis's funeral home were crammed in at the top. They were written in Spanish. A FedEx cardboard box labeled "human ashes" had been postmarked in San Ysidro in July 2008. Had my mother really saved all of this stuff? She'd wanted nothing to do with those ashes.

In the same box were Mom's receipts for legitimate-looking prescriptions for lithium, Zoloft, Seroquel, and Klonopin, purchased at her local pharmacy, and six unsealed envelopes containing prescription drugs, some of which were benzodiazepines, each one labeled in what was unmistakably Atlantis's handwriting: "Valium (weakest)," a two-milligram pill; "Valium (strongest)," a ten-milligram pill; "Ativan (strongest)," two two-milligram pills, one partly crumbled; "Klonopin (strongest)," three two-milligram pills; and one milligram of "Xanax (very strong)."

.

I drove out to visit the Lancaster County Forensic Center on Spring Valley Road, whose staff redirected me to the city's Government Center on Queen Street. There I was able to access the police and toxicology reports of my mother's death. I'd never had any desire to see these reports before. I wanted to find out exactly what combination of drugs had killed my mother. The drug-filled envelopes I'd found suggested that my sister—or someone—might have made it easier for my mother to commit suicide by sharing drugs that she hadn't been prescribed and giving her instructions.

My mother's toxicology reports had been done twice: once in December, and again in February. Lithium, Seroquel, Klonopin, and benzodiazepines were among the drugs found in her blood. I remembered the care she used to take in applying her lipstick and blue eyeliner. Sometimes medication made her hands tremble, and when my sister and I were teenagers, Nancy called her the Clown.

·

I also reached out to the German Gentleman and told him I was writing a book about Atlantis. I asked if he had any memories of her that he'd be willing to share. "I remember your sister well," he wrote back.

> *I knew her only for a very short time, but she was very dear to my heart. She visit me in Mexico and she wanted to move together with me. We called each other Bonny and Clyde for fun, we both understood each other very well.*

> *I am traveling right now in Europe, but soon I will write a little more.*

I didn't doubt Atlantis's charisma, her secret power: she'd managed to become Gretchen's "muse" after just one in-person meeting, BFFs with Guitar Girl, dear to the German Gentleman's heart after one weekend together when she was going through hell. Misfits tended to be in love with Atlantis.

·

Then I heard from him again:

I believe I told you about your sister wanting to move to Mexico with me. We called each other Bonnie and Clyde, understanding each other very well. What I didn't tell you, was things Atlantis were worry about. Not knowing your sistier well enough, how much truth or what real reason were behind it and how much drugs were part of it, you probably know this better, what to make out of it and most of it you most likely know any way.

Atlantis told me, that she was in trouble, something with description of drugs, going to court and that she was worry about here life. It sounded like the possibility being killed. She said I have to take care of few things in the US and in few weeks she will be back in Mexico with me. She said, don't be surprise to hear about my death. I ask her to stay, not knowing what was really going on, but she left.

After that I received only few emails from Atlantis. So more I was shocked to hear from you months later, that Atlantis died. I am sorry, it must be still so hard to think about your sister. Her music had so much feelings, including the deep sadness.

I hope I will have the chance to read your book about Atlantis.

The very best,
[Name redacted]

I asked if he'd ever heard of death certificates or autopsy reports in Tijuana being forged, or of a different person's IDs left with an unidentified body. He wrote back the next day:

> *I didn't know that about your sister and that she was back in Mexico. I do remember her saying, don't be surprise, if you do hear, I am dead. It seems to me, she was worry about her life and the charges made agains her in the US. Also she was talking about to disappear, Mexico or further south. With all the info you may could be right, that she is in hiding and living a new life under a different name. Also she was talking about false passports. Somehow I like to believe, with all the sadness and worries, she was to much into life.*

I placed an order on Amazon for an anthology of poetry that the German Gentleman had edited and published. It included a poem he'd written for Atlantis.

.

I called First Adult Therapist and introduced myself as the sister of her former patient Atlantis Black. I told her that I was writing a book and asked if she might be willing to meet and talk to me.

"Where is Atlantis?" she asked.

I told her the story. I was aware, I said, that my sister had harassed her, and that Atlantis's last phone calls had been to her and her husband. Did she remember listening to those messages?

She said that this was the first she'd heard about the disappearance, and that under the circumstances she didn't think she could talk to me. Would I send her a letter formally requesting an interview? "You know," she said, "you're just a voice at the end of the line."

I wrote the letter, but I never heard back from her.

.

The next time I called Gretchen, I left her a voicemail saying that I realized I'd been asking the wrong questions. I said I didn't believe that Atlantis died the way the Tijuana reports said, either; and I wanted to know if Atlantis was still alive, and if so, if Gretchen knew how to be in touch with her.

She called me back immediately—from a different number than the one I'd called—and we talked for nearly two hours. She was adamant about not being recorded, and said that if I was recording the call, nothing she said would be admissible in "a court of law." I told her I wasn't recording her, which was the truth. I never wanted to hear that voice again.

Was it possible, I asked, that my sister might still be alive? She didn't think so—but then, later in the conversation, she said that Atlantis might be living in the United States under another name. At any rate, she said that she knew that Atlantis hadn't died the way the Tijuana reports had said, and that the body found in the hotel room hadn't been hers. She said that anyone could buy anything in Tijuana, and that though the police report was real—someone had died in a hotel room, with "some guy lying on the floor"—she knew it wasn't Atlantis or the truth about what happened. And even if it *had* been my sister's body, the idea that her death had been caused by a heroin overdose was simply impossible. The toxicology report, she said, had shown only trace amounts of opiates, not enough to kill a person.

So she *had* seen the reports.

She claimed that she was frequently called in to court to give evidence as an "attorney," and commented that if Atlantis had known her "rights," she never would have gotten into that legal mess.

She mentioned that she knew many people who'd committed suicide—she herself had "a room full of ashes"—but Atlantis was the only person she ever knew to "disappear." She said that Atlantis hated Mexico—and I realized that nearly every other word out of her mouth was "hate." She added that after Atlantis disappeared and was presumed dead, someone texted a message to her from Atlantis's cell phone that said in Spanish: "Are you gay?" Gretchen said she'd called the person back and said that this was a cell phone that had been stolen from a dead American woman, and that the person had better "drop the phone." Gretchen claimed that when she'd received that text, she'd wondered if Atlantis had really been the sender, and if she'd sent it to let Gretchen know—in secret code—that she was still alive. But Gretchen said she didn't really believe this.

She claimed that there never was any Report of Death of an American Abroad. I told her that, in fact, I'd filed one on Atlantis's behalf the previous year, in 2014. (I'd filed it in order to use the Freedom of Information Act and get the DEA's report on Atlantis.) This made her laugh. How had I managed that? I said I'd used the Mexican death certificate, which she also found funny. She volunteered that she knew that "ashes are white and powdery, not brown" the way Atlantis's had appeared in a photo she'd somehow seen of Leah and me spreading them in the desert.

I told her that I'd viewed autopsy photos and had identified
Atlantis positively; she asked me how I'd seen them. I said the consulate had emailed them to me; she said no embassy would email
autopsy photos, and that I must have been communicating with
someone who wasn't from the embassy at all, and that the reports
my mother had received in the mail were absolutely wrong—she
knew that as a fact—and that I was right not to trust any of the
information coming out of Mexico.

She volunteered that suicide notes "only happen in movies,"
but she said that she knew that my mother had "killed herself"
because she was very depressed, lived alone, was older, and it was
a holiday. And she volunteered one more odd piece of information: that before my mother died, she had asked Gretchen about "a
particular drug." What drug? Gretchen wouldn't say. Impulsively, I
asked Gretchen if she had killed my mother. She laughed and said,
"What, are you crazy, lady?"

.

It was almost too much for me. I called the Ephrata police and
told them about the conversation. I named Gretchen—and possibly Atlantis Black—as people who might have forged my mother's
suicide note. The police said they would re-examine my mother's
death for evidence of foul play. To my knowledge, nothing ever
came of any investigation.

I went so far as to tell my story to the FBI; they said that both
my mother's death and my sister's disappearance were out of their
jurisdiction.

.

In September 2015, a friend introduced me over email to Dr. Jonathan Hayes, chief medical examiner of the City of New York, who'd spent eight months identifying bodies after the attacks on September 11. (In his spare time, he writes books about serial killers.) The friend who made the introduction felt that seven years was too long for me to be in uncertainty and denial. I'd avoided telling people I was still searching for evidence that the Tijuana reports were wrong, but some of them knew anyway. The reports were sketchy, of course, riddled with mistakes and omissions, but I didn't want people to worry about my state of mind, or to doubt my sanity. I was ashamed to have wasted years obsessing over details and typos, of doing everything I could to avoid the truth—if I could settle on what the truth was.

I told Dr. Hayes that my sister had had a stalker who called herself a forensic psychologist, and that I doubted the veracity of at least some of the reports of my sister's death. Dr. Hayes asked a colleague, Raphael, a forensics expert who'd done some of his medical training in Mexico, to make a full translation of the reports. And he offered to read them and help me to understand and accept them.

It took Raphael a few weeks to complete the translation of one of Atlantis's toxicology reports—a report that the Tijuana consulate had no record of having ever been done. Dr. Hayes forwarded me the completed translation. It stated that there hadn't been any alcohol in Atlantis's system when she died. The only substance for which her blood had tested positive was opiates. Dr. Hayes sent me this information with a message:

I'm afraid there are no conclusions to be leaped to from it.

And I saw that Dr. Hayes had copied me—deliberately or accidentally, I wasn't sure—on his personal correspondence with Raphael:

> *I've had a steady stream of emails from Betsy, and I think she
> may be a bit obsessive. I suspect she needs a therapist more than
> she needs a forensic pathologist. I think it might be better if I
> handle the direct dealing with her—I feel sorry for her, but I
> think she does need "handling." I think it's an example of the
> myth of "closure" in certain deaths.*

I agreed to meet Dr. Hayes in person for coffee at the NoMad, a hip
Manhattan hotel on Twenty-Eighth and Broadway. Dr. Hayes had
a wax-tipped mustache, and marvelous tattoos on his forearms—a
line from *The Waste Land*, another from Shakespeare, and a sleeve
of moths. The servers seemed to know and like him.

I thanked him for helping me, and let him know that I understood "closure" was a myth for most people. When my father died, I
told him, his death had receded into the past and taken up a smaller
amount of space. What complicated things for me about my sister's
death was that I couldn't get a simple answer about what literally *had*
happened. Probably "solving the mystery" wouldn't have brought any
more "closure" than if Atlantis (and my mother) had died with no
mystery or weirdness. Still, most survivors do get a set of concrete
facts to deal with. Or not deal with. It would have been easier to put
something certain behind me—what, exactly, *did* I have to accept?

I told him that I suspected that Gretchen might have forged
one of the toxicology reports (the one involving alcohol, which

supposedly proved that Atlantis couldn't have died of an opiate overdose because the amount in her blood wasn't enough to kill a person) and mailed it to my mother (or left it in her house). He laughed. So what if she had? When he'd seen the report, he'd thought that translating it had been a waste of his colleague's time and my money.

By Tijuana standards, he told me, the investigation into my sister's death had actually been pretty thorough. The bump on her cranium that had caused a brain hemorrhage was most likely the result of her having fallen facedown on the floor after a heroin overdose. The pancreatic hemorrhage was also most likely the result of an overdose. Dr. Hayes couldn't say with certainty that the body was my sister's, but he did say he didn't think I was crazy. "You've inlaid your obsession into the frame of writing a book," he wrote to me in October 2015. "But mostly I don't think you are crazy because I very much want you not to be crazy."

.

I still have questions. At the time of my sister's disappearance, she had driven away everyone to whom she mattered. Is there anyone now who could tell me what really happened to her? That is, anyone who could be believed?

I never tried to meet my sister at the Louvre because I knew she wouldn't—couldn't—be there. And I also dreaded that she might actually show up. If she were still alive in the year I write this, she'd be forty-two. But she'll be thirty-one forever.

My own life has been shaped by what I inherited: most of all, my sister's story. I'm still living off of her fortune.

ACKNOWLEDGMENTS

I am most grateful to my editor, Masie Cochran, and to my agent, Mary Krienke, for their belief in this book; and to all at Tin House for their hard work, especially to Craig Popelars, Nanci McCloskey, Molly Templeton, Diane Chonette, Jeremy Cruz, Elizabeth DeMeo, Alyssa Ogi, Yashwina Canter, Anne Horowitz, and Allison Dubinsky.

To Tim Adams, Bettina Heffner, Leah Jackson, and Elizabeth MacNeill Misner: thank you for your generous spirits and courageous love.

To my first readers of early drafts, especially to David Gates, Rachel Paige King, and Paul La Farge: you helped bring this book to life through your tireless questions and encouragement over the years.

Thanks to the T. S. Eliot House for providing generous support during the editing process.

Thanks also to Buddy, Stephen Byler, Jane Carr, Christopher Castellani, Ben Downing, Sacha Evans, Nick Flynn, Jennifer Gilmore, Michael Greenberg, Dr. Jonathan Hayes, Kit Heffner,

Amy Hempel, Dr. John Heussy, Chloe Honum, Tara Howley, Lee Clay Johnson, Jus'Mayne, Colleen Kane, Kelly Loudenberg, Margot Lurie, Ricardo Maldonado, Deirdre McNamer, Catherine Meehan, Ryan Murphy, Lynn Phillips, Orianna Riley, Wendy Salinger, Bernard Schwartz, Erika Seidman, Jesse Sheidlower, Dr. Stanley Siegel, Wylie Stecklow, Ginger Strand, Catherine Talese, Amanda Turner, Heidy Valbuena, Elizabeth Van Meter, Remy Weber, Jonathan Wells, Joel Whitney, and Rebecca Wolff.

Thanks to my teachers, and to my creative writing students, for giving me hope.